274 FRA 1995

Frank, Isnard Wilhelm.
A concise history of the
mediaeval church.

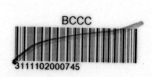
DEMCO

A Concise History of the Mediaeval Church

A CONCISE HISTORY OF THE MEDIAEVAL CHURCH

Isnard Wilhelm Frank

Continuum • New York

1996

The Continuum Publishing Company
370 Lexington Avenue
New York, NY 10017

Translated by John Bowden from the second edition
of the German *Kirchengeschichte des Mittelalters*,
published 1990 by Patmos Verlag, Düsseldorf.

© Patmos Verlag, Düsseldorf, 1984, 1990

Translation © John Bowden 1995

Printed in the United States of America

Library of Congress Cataloging-in-Publication Data

Frank, Isnard Wilhelm.
    [Kirchengeschichte des Mittelalters.   English]
    A concise history of the mediaeval church / Isnard Wilhelm Frank.
        p.   cm.
    Includes bibliographical references and index.
    ISBN 0-8264-0828-1
    1. Church history — Middle Ages, 600–1500. I. Title.
BR252.F7813   1995
274 — dc20   95–10867
                                                                              CIP

Contents

Contents

Preface

With so many urgent questions that need to be asked about the role and place of the church in modern secularized society, what the mediaeval church was like might seem to be of merely marginal interest. Indeed, there are those who find this church a burden, a degeneration of witness to Christian salvation in history which is difficult to understand. But that would be a superficial view. Rather than standing back from the mediaeval church and criticizing it, we should try to understand how it proclaimed, lived out and expressed 'salvation' in significant social structures. We need to understand how the shape of the church and of Christian society was conditioned by these structures.

That is the aim of this book. Because of the limited space available, the material has to be presented in a concentrated form. However, it is not enough just to give indispensable facts; it is also important to bring out the leading ideas and formative forces of the period. That makes the arrangement of the material more important than the particular selection of facts, which is always open to discussion.

Since the mediaeval church is unthinkable without the papacy, this institution provides as it were the backbone for the book. After all, Western Christendom, with which it will be dealing, found its unity in the papacy. The material will not be treated in strict chronological order, but individual topics will be discussed in chapters and sections, as they fit in with this basic pattern. This arrangement should be noted in working through the material and coming to grips with the issues. Particular attention should be paid to sections 3 and 4 of Chapter I, which highlight the structures of piety and church order which were to remain fundamental for the whole of the Middle Ages.

I

The Appropriation and Transformation of Christianity

Mediaeval Christianity in Europe was transmitted and shaped by new peoples. Along with the Celts in the extreme West and the Slavs in the East, the various German tribes were particularly significant here. In the course of a large-scale movement, the historical details of which can no longer be ascertained, and which is simply referred to as the 'migrations', from the first century onwards these tribes had come within the horizons of the Graeco-Roman world. Individual groups were incorporated into the empire as allies and by exploiting the weakness and centrifugal tendencies of the later empire they established kingdoms and gained recognition from the emperor.

In the long run, of these Germanic kingdoms only that of the Franks, which had been forged by the successful military king Clovis (481–511), proved to be a lasting one. Clovis' successors drove the West Goths out of Aquitania, incorporated the kingdom of Burgundy into the Frankish realm and conquered the Thuringians and Alemanns. The Carolingians continued the expansion and incorporated Bavaria, Thuringia, Saxony and the Langobards into the Frankish empire. By the end of Charlemagne's reign, all the Germanic tribes except for the Anglo-Saxons and the Germans of Scandinavia had been incorporated into the Frankish empire.

In this political framework which was becoming established, Christianity turned into Western Christendom. As a result it slowly became alienated from the Christianity of the Eastern Roman empire, which was caught up in a process of progressive Hellenization. Various reasons can be given for this. From the start linguistic differences played a significant role and were always a key factor in the split of the empire into a Greek-speaking East and a Latin-speaking West from 395 onwards.

The new peoples in new areas were first presented with the Roman provincial Christianity of late antiquity. They took this over in a long historical process, with variations depending on their mentality, and adapted the traditional church order to their forms of socialization and social needs. The spiritual and organizational foundations which came into being in this process remained fundamental for the Middle Ages. They first of all led in almost a straight line to a church dominated by the king and the nobility. They had a decisive effect on the church's reaction to the 'Germanic distortions', namely in the 'Gregorian reform', which culminated in the papal church of the high Middle Ages. The same is true of piety (cf. c below).

1. The Christianization of the Germans, Celts and Slavs

The process of Christianization extended over a period of around a thousand years. This means that there were differences in the nature of the mission, which extended from what were initially individual conversions, through mass conversion as the institutions of the Roman empire became Christianized, to forced conversions and missions with the sword in the high Middle Ages and at the beginning of the late Middle Ages.

The Germanic tribes involved in the migrations turned to Christianity in late Christian antiquity. Thus in the course of the fourth century the East Goths, who had settled in the Balkans, became Christians. They were influenced by the variants of Arian belief prevailing at the imperial court of the time, and this influence continued even after the imperial church had again turned away from Arianism. The West Goths, Vandals, Burgundians and Langobards were also Arian.

We also have to understand this Arianism in political terms. The Arian church with its tribal structure helped people to stand apart from the conquered indigenous population by their confession, so that they kept their own identity. But such a policy of 'apartheid' also represented a refusal to accept the culture of late antiquity, which was still alive in the ecclesiastical institutions of the Romanized population. So these Germanic kingdoms failed to exert any lasting historical influence. Granted, under King Reccared (586–601) the West Goths in Spain in 589 accepted Catholic Christianity for their subjects. However, the Spanish church with its ancient institutions and traditions was prevented from having any long-term and effective formative influence on the rising West by the Arab conquest (711).

This role fell to the Franks, who had been united under Clovis. They found their way to the Catholic Church without going through Arianism. After a victory over the Alemanns, Clovis had himself baptized, probably in 498 by the Gallo-Roman Bishop Remigius of Reims. Numerous Frankish noblemen went over to Christianity with their king. The indigenous episcopate celebrated the entry of the pagan Franks into the Gallo-Roman church as if Clovis were a second Constantine.

(a) Mission in the early mediaeval Frankish kingdom

In the course of the fifth century, probably the whole of the indigenous population of the old Roman provinces of Gaul had become Christian. However, on the frontiers, on the lands alongside the Rhine, in Switzerland and the foothills of the Alps, this was not the case. Here only remnants of a Christianity which had not yet become established survived the different Germanic settlements. Only with the stabilization of conditions and the conversion of the Frankish upper class to Christianity did the Christian communities begin to be reinforced and to expand. Initially it was the bishops who had been responsible for what missions had developed or were being made possible again. However, increasingly individual clergy (monks and hermits) emerged who had a personal relationship with a bishop and who were active in mission as ascetic miracle workers and itinerant preachers, like Goar, Wendelin, Disibod, Fridolin and Trudpert. Churches founded in the flat land by kings, noblemen and bishops supported the activity of the ascetic itinerant preachers.

We should note the movement from west to east in the expansion of Christianity into the Germanic sphere of settlement. Monasteries and churches under the direct control of bishops helped to reorganize the communities which lay further east until these were strong enough to form bases beyond the Rhine. The Christianization of Bavaria first took place from northern Italy. In the course of the eighth century Bavaria was incorporated into the Frankish mission.

All in all, one important factor must be remembered. Becoming Christian always also meant being incorporated into the Frankish empire. Missions were planned and churches and monasteries founded under the protection of the Frankish kings and served to enlarge their realm. The other side of this missionary policy was a politically motivated resistance to the acceptance of Christianity. This resistance was crushed by force.

At the end of the seventh century monks increasingly emerged as missionaries. They combined a missionary and apostolic zeal with monastic asceticism and made monasticism an important agent in the Christianization of the European interior. Two interconnected reasons may have been crucial here: first the long disintegration of the bishop's church as a result of the proprietary church system (see below 4, b), and secondly the interest of the local nobility in gaining and reinforcing influence on their own monasteries. The main figures in monastic mission were initially Iro-Scottish and Gallo-Frankish monks, and later Anglo-Saxon and Frankish monks.

(i) The Iro-Scottish and Gallo-Frankish mission

The Iro-Scottish missionaries were monks who came to the European continent from the British Isles. There, especially in Ireland, a Celtic church had taken shape in an amazingly short time.

The beginnings of the Christianization of the Celts are largely shrouded in darkness. The mysterious figure of St Patrick dominates the tradition. This Christian Briton, carried off by pirates to Ireland, became a monk after escaping to the mainland. He then returned to the Irish as a missionary bishop. Between 430 and 460 Patrick managed to persuade the heads of the clans to accept Christianity. The Irish church developed along monastic lines, i.e. through an association between clans and monasteries. So the monasteries took the place of churches with clergy under a bishop and assumed their task of pastoral care. Hence the description 'Celtic monastic church'. Because of their pastoral role, Irish monks also had a positive attitude to education and zealously accepted Latin culture as it was introduced to them.

The missionary zeal which soon extended to Great Britain and the European continent had monastic and ascetic roots. In ascetic denial of the world and voluntary penance, monks left their homeland and founded monasteries and cells abroad (*peregrinatio pro Christo*). This monastic ideal was also alive in other monastic centres. However, the legends of a later time make most of the itinerant monks Iro-Scottish.

The monasteries of the foreign monks were encouraged by the local rulers and the Merovingian kings. One of the most famous Iro-Scottish monasteries was Luxeuil in the Western Vosges, founded by Columba the Younger. Columba later travelled to northern Italy, where he died in 615 in the monastery of Bobbio, which he had founded. His circle also included Gallus, Magnus, Eustasius and others, who were active in the foothills of the Alps.

In the Iro-Scottish monasteries of the Merovingian kingdom there was a significant mixing of the old indigenous Gallo-Roman monasticism with Celtic monasticism. Whereas the older Gallo-Romanic monastery was still largely the concern of the Romanic population and the local ruler, the new Gallo-Celtic monastery, being Gallo-Frankish, had closer connections with the Franks and the royal house. These monks became involved in Frankish missionary activity, which was carried on for political ends. St Pirmin (died 753) can be seen as the dominant figure of Gallo-Frankish monasticism. He was active above all among the Alemanns and contributed to the consolidation of Christianization by founding monasteries and monastic cells.

(ii) The Anglo-Saxon mission

From the middle of the eighth century, Anglo-Saxon missionaries joined the Iro-Scottish and Gallo-Frankish missionaries, often in a tense rivalry; they finally gave a new stamp to monasticism on the European continent and developed new forms of church organization.

The Anglo-Saxon monks came from Great Britain. After the departure of the Romans, remnants of the Christian communities in Roman Britain managed to survive, and in conjunction with the Irish missionaries they had a growing influence on the population. This was interrupted and halted by the Anglo-Saxons and Jutes, who invaded from Scandinavia around 450. The decisive impetus for the Christianization of the Anglo-Saxons came from Rome. In 596 Gregory the Great sent Augustine, the head of the Roman monastery of St Andrew, to England with some monks. In some tension with the Celtic-Irish forms of Christianity, a mission church was established, following Roman church order. The Synod of Whitby in 664 decided in favour of it.

Orientation on Roman custom primarily affected church order, i.e. bishops were the heads of churches and individual dioceses were brought together under a metropolitan. Theodore of Tarsus, who came from Rome (669–690), became the organizer of the Anglo-Saxon church as Archbishop of Canterbury.

Although Roman church order was adopted, as among the Celts it was the monasteries which shaped spiritual and cultural life and the missionary apostolate. Just how indispensable the monastic element was is clear from the establishment of monasteries in the places where bishops resided. The 'minster' is a typical product of this alliance of the bishop's church modelled on the early church and the Roman church with the Celtic Anglo-Saxon monastic church. Thus the bishop became an abbot and the abbot a bishop.

Christianization and the appropriation of Christianity proved successful. For the beginning of the eighth century saw the 'golden age' of the Anglo-Saxon church, in which culture blossomed. It was developed by monks, who were even more strongly interested in 'academic education' than the Irish. The most famous of them was the Venerable Bede (died 735). The Rule of Benedict as a symbol of allegiance to the Roman model must also have been made a binding norm in Anglo-Saxon monasticism at a very early stage.

The monastic ideal of the *peregrinatio pro Christo* made the Anglo-Saxon monks willing servants of the missionary apostolate. On the European continent their mission sphere was the new territory among the Frisians, Thuringians and Saxons which hitherto had hardly been opened up by the church. This mission, too, was sponsored by the Franks or the Carolingians, who extended their influence to the right bank of the Rhine.

The best-known and most distinguished figure in the Anglo-Saxon activity on the European continent is Winfrid Boniface, the 'Apostle of the Germans'. Born between 671 and 673, he had grown up in Anglo-Saxon monasticism, i.e. in a combination of asceticism, education and missionary activity. After a first and probably not very successful period of activity among the Frisians in 716, in 718 Boniface made a new start. His way took him first to Rome, to be given a missionary charge by the pope. Royal protection may also have been linked with the papal commission. On 15 May 719 Pope Gregory II gave him the task of carrying on a mission among the 'wild peoples of Germania'. As an expression of his allegiance to Rome at that time, following the model of other Anglo-Saxon missionaries, he adopted the name of the Roman martyr Boniface. From then on Boniface deliberately followed the Roman model and Roman instructions, and all his life was in correspondence with Rome. In 722 he was consecrated bishop in Rome, gave an oath of loyalty to the pope, and thus entered into a special relationship of dependence on the Bishop of Rome as his metropolitan. As an expression of this bond, in 732 he was given the pallium. Finally, in 738 Gregory III named him 'Ambassador of St Peter for Germania' with a brief to establish a church province.

However, the political situation did not favour the implementation of this plan, with which Boniface combined a reform and reorganization of the Frankish church along Roman lines. Charles Martel (714–41), at that time the real ruler of the Frankish empire, had no time for it, nor did his bishops. Countless conflicts were programmed into the ambitious plans of the Anglo-Saxon Boniface, which overshadowed his work, and in the end they proved too much for him.

For a time Boniface evaded the conflicts and contented himself with founding monasteries and with missionary activity. For a short period he found support from the dukes of Bavaria, and between 738 and 739 was at least able to sketch out a church order. He attempted to attach the itinerant bishops in the country to episcopal monasteries, as was customary in his Anglo-Saxon homeland. Such episcopal 'minsters' were established in Salzburg, Freising, Regensburg and Passau.

After the death of Charles Martel in 741, Boniface was able to return to the Frankish empire. In Charles' successors Carloman and Pepin he found temporary supporters of his cause. A series of imperial synods enacted laws which did away with the excesses of the proprietary church system and limited the arbitrariness of those who controlled it. The idea of church organization east of the Rhine was also taken up. Boniface was to be metropolitan of the new church province with his seat in Cologne. Episcopal monasteries were planned in Büraburg, Erfurt, Würzburg and Eichstatt.

However, further tensions in church policy prevented the implementation of the plan. What had been begun came to a standstill and Boniface was assigned only the diocese of Mainz (747). He found himself increasingly at the periphery of church affairs. At the end of his life, as an old man he was again active among the Frisians, perhaps as interim Bishop of Utrecht. On a confirmation visit he was killed by pagan robbers on 5 June 754 at Dokkum (he is buried in Fulda cathedral).

(b) Mission in the Carolingian empire

The frontier regions were the geographical focal points of political expansion and Christianization under Charlemagne (768–814) and Louis the Pious (814–40). In the south-east these were the Ostmark (Lower Austria) and the Carinthian Mark (Styria-Carinthia), and in the north-east above all Saxony.

It is important to note the political framework outlined in II, 1, a and b when reading this and the next section. In the course of the ninth century there was also strong missionary expansion from Constantinople through the Balkans as far as Russia. At times this was in competition with the Roman and Frankish mission. The mission of the brothers Cyril (Constantine, died 884) and Methodius (died 869) to the Slavs was affected and hindered by this.

The Christianization of the Saxons caused great difficulties. The powerful resistance which kept flaring up again was primarily of a political kind. Resistance to the assimilation into the Frankish empire associated with Christianization was organized by Widukind, whom Charlemagne attempted to break in numerous Saxon wars fought with great harshness, as is shown by the massacre at Verdun (782). With the conversion of Widukind to Christianity in 785 the common will to resistance was broken. However, local revolts continued into the ninth century.

Those behind the Christianization associated with the expansion of the Frankish empires were the diocesan churches and monasteries of the Frankish church. Under the influence of Anglo-Saxon discipline, in the meantime a new generation of Frankish clergy and monks had grown up, like Chrodegang of Metz and Fulrad of St Denis. The newly strengthened institutions put their personnel and resources at the disposal of the Franks in a kind of partnership. So the new churches that were founded were rapidly consolidated. In addition to monasteries like Corbie and Werden, from the beginning these also included churches modelled on the Anglo-Saxon minsters. Such churches were founded in Münster, Osnabrück, Paderborn, Hamburg, Bremen, Verdun, Minden, Hildesheim and Halberstadt.

The diocese had again become necessary as a centre of church activity and organization. The Carolingian reform laws attempted to remove the excesses of the proprietary church system in which the church was controlled by the local rulers and to prevent the decay of the church into local institutions. Well-defined districts and clear responsibilities were needed in connection with the public functions assigned to the bishop. So under Charlemagne the church organization of the Frankish church was also completed. Clearly defined dioceses were brought together into metropolitan groupings. Within the territory of the later German empire, Mainz was elevated to an archbishopric between 780 and 782, Cologne in 795 and Salzburg in 798.

So from the seventh to the ninth century there was a notable expansion of Christianity among the Germans and on the frontiers already among the Slavs, coupled with a rapid consolidation of church institutions. This success allows us to infer that early mediaeval Christianity, which from a later perspective seems so archaic and primitive, had a certain inner force. Of course we must not fail to observe that the political pressure exerted by the Frankish empire and the protection that it offered contributed to this success. It should also be noted that the mission field had been marked out clearly and that the available forces were not dissipated. The restless ascetic urge to travel drew missionaries to Jerusalem and into the East, but the way there had been barred by the Arabs. Moreover their advance through North Africa to Spain in the course of the seventh and eighth centuries had transformed the Mediterranean from being an internal sea binding together the Graeco-Roman world into a barrier which led the people of Europe in the early Middle Ages to penetrate and cultivate the European interior.

(c) Mission within the framework of the church of the German empire

During the course of the ninth century, at first missionary expansion was paralysed. This was a result of the internal collapse of the great Frankish empire and the countless external threats of the time: the invasions of the Vikings/Normans in the north and west, the Hungarians in the south-east and the Saracens in the south-west. To the west, the central area of the Frankish realm fell apart into local domains with the progressive feudalization. However, there was some consolidation in the eastern part of the empire during the tenth century. The tribes combined to form the 'German empire'. With this internal reinforcement the pressure to expand also revived. The direction was obvious: expansion eastwards, to achieve the Christianization and Germanization of the Slavs. This seems to have been carried out without any problems in present-day Carinthia and among the Slavs on the upper reaches of the Main (the bishopric of Bamberg was founded in 1007 by Henry II).

The Slavs in Holstein, Mecklenburg and in the areas east of the Elbe were Germanized by force, in a mission with the sword. The most important base for the Christianization of the Slavs of the Elbe was Magdeburg (established as an archbishopric by Otto the Great in 968). In founding this archbishopric the emperor was pursuing ambitious plans. Magdeburg was to be the centre for the Christianization of Poland, in connection with which Poland was to be incorporated into the empire. However, in the end the transnational idea of a Christian Roman empire led to a 'national' solution. Poland became an independent kingdom in the framework of Western Christendom (the church province of Gnesen was established in 1000). The same is true of Hungary (the church province of Gran was established in 1001) and the Scandinavian countries (the archbishopric of Lund was established in 1004 and that of Drontheim in 1152).

Initially it had been planned that these countries, too, should be incorporated into the church of the empire. Thus Archbishop Adalbert of Bremen (who died in 1079), taking up the work of St Ansgar (who died in 865), was pursuing ambitious plans with a view to the Christianization of Denmark, Sweden and Norway. Bremen was to be the seat of a metropolitan for a church province embracing the whole of Scandinavia. Pilgrim of Passau (who died in 991) had planned the same thing for the south-eastern area of the Danube. From a nationalistic point of view, Christianization came too early for the Czechs. It had been in process since the ninth century and was still firmly tied to the West. The diocese of Prague established in 973 remained dependent on Mainz until 1344.

The Christianization of the Prussians by the Teutonic Orders in the thirteenth cenutry also led to their Germanization, strongly reinforced by the settling of German colonists. Lithuania was the last European country to turn to Christianity in the Middle Ages after the baptism of Prince Jagiello. In 1386 he married the Piast heiress Hedwig and became king of Poland-Lithuania as Ladislaus II.

The reform orders of the twelfth century (Cistercians, Premonstratensians and Augustinian Canons) played a prominent role in the mission and establishment of Christianity in the areas mentioned. Some dioceses like Havelberg, Brandenburg, Schwerin and Ratzeburg were initially Premonstratensian episcopal monasteries. In the thirteenth and fourteenth centuries the new mendicant orders played an important role in mission. Secular clergy, cathedral chapters and bishops had again delegated missionary and pastoral tasks to the monks.

2. Motives for conversion and methods of mission

Ultimately the turning of the Germans towards Christianity in the course of the early Middle Ages is to be understood as an anonymous process which lasted many generations. Bishops' churches, monasteries and other church institutions were merely the consolidation of what had been achieved. Of the mixture of motives which prompted conversion, historically speaking, only those which are visible can be listed. Here we might start with the social order. In early mediaeval society only the nobility had political freedom, so all attempts at conversion had to be directed at this class. Here the most important figures were the kings. If they were converted, the die had been cast. It was then only a matter of time before the lesser nobility followed them. The dependent lower classes simply had to follow their rulers' change of religion. So the important thing was to motivate the nobility to conversion. There were various possible motives. Here kinship with Christian families and marriage to their princesses also played a role, but what proved most important were contacts with the indigenous Christian population. That was especially true of the Franks, who had settled in the old Roman provinces of Gaul.

The Christian communities of the land had long been very important for political, social, cultural and religious life. United in faith, doctrine and life, and disciplined by law, they were superior to the pagan Germans in many respects. This manifest organizational, spiritual, moral and cultural superiority was a key factor. Clovis depended on the support of the bishops of the Gallican church to administer his kingdom. Ultimately it made political sense to accept the faith of this church, to draw on its religious and spiritual power and participate in a higher level of culture. To take such a step was not too much to ask of the pagan Germans, because to convert to Christianity did not mean turning their backs on their own religion. For both the Christian faith of late antiquity and pagan religion were understood against the background of a political sense of religion.

The primitive archaic religion of the agricultural society of Germans, Celts and Slavs aimed at the earthly and heavenly well-being of individual and community. The blessings of the gods carried obligations with them: observation of the customs and usages handed down from antiquity. Cult and rites had enormous significance.

As state religion and popular religion, the Christianity of late antiquity had long taken on the features of a religion of cultic observances, involving the precise observance of divine commandments and the careful performance of cultic regulations. Thus the religious and cultic understanding of religion and religious cultic practice were the bridge from pagan to Christian religion in the transition from late antiquity to the early Middle Ages. The religion of the churches of late antiquity with its many sacred actions, rites and customs had an extensive catalogue of prescribed behaviour to offer which provided norms and stability for morality and life. In this respect the Christianity of late antiquity went beyond pagan religion.

However, in their archaic agricultural society, too, the Celts, Germans and Slavs sought to provide norms and legal security for the social life of the community through morals and customs. The transition to Christianity did not tear them away from a religion of cultic observances, but enabled them to make these observances deeper and richer. So in many respects, at the first stage of its reception Christianity was not much more than a continuation of the old customs under new auspices. Though many new features had been added, the content remained the same; it was only as it were the brand name that had been changed. The more powerful God of the Christians took the place of the gods who had hitherto been called upon. The conversion to Christianity amounted to a change of gods, and there had also been changes from one tribal deity to another among the Germans at an early stage. Thus the settlement in Gaul brought with it pressure to accept the god worshipped there and made him appear the more powerful.

This view is also reflected in the conversion testimonies. Thus Gregory of Tours reports that before his conversion, Clovis had taken counsel with his great men. These had replied: 'Let us leave our mortal gods and turn to the immortal God of the Christians.' We need to consider the basic content of this fictitious conversation. By 'immortal God' the Germans understood what both individual and collective saw as the guarantor of a comprehensive salvation to whom the '*tils ars ok fridar*' (good year and peace) belonged. The power of the God of the Christians also displayed itself in success in battles. Gregory of Tours makes Clovis pray before his battle with the Alemanns: 'If you now grant me victory over these my enemies and I experience your power, then I will believe in you and be baptized.' Other miracles and mighty acts of the God of the Christians played a role here. The best-known testimony was the destruction by Boniface of the Donar oak, a clan sanctuary at Geismar.

Given this starting point and the mixture of motives for conversion, the many questions about the missionary methods used in Christianization prove superfluous. The lower classes simply changed religion along with their lords. The proprietary church controlled by the local lord was the home in which they became familiar with the Christian cult and the new rites. So we have to imagine the external acceptance of Christianity as a rapid event (mass baptisms). By contrast, inner appropriation was a long-drawn-out process in which solidly pagan notions could only be eliminated laboriously or fused into the newly accepted faith. What determined praxis may have been a mixture of pagan notions and Christian formulae. Pastoral instruction was aimed above all at teaching the basic Christian prayers (the Lord's Prayer and the Creed) and encouraging the practice of confession, which also involved learning a catalogue of duties.

3. Characteristics of early mediaeval piety

Germans, Celts and Slavs went over to Christianity and allowed themselves to be shaped by it. But we must not overlook the reverse process. The new Christians shaped the tradition in accordance with their ideas and needs. The result of this history of appropriation is early mediaeval piety, which had a long influence.

(a) No Christian church community

One fact which is important for the whole of the Middle Ages, that there was no Christian church community, needs to be considered in connection with the spread of the proprietary church, the church controlled by the local lord. This led to the disintegration and transformation of the former bishops' churches and the communities around them. This process of transformation eventually resulted in the mediaeval parish, which was primarily an administrative unit.

To judge from its beginnings in the early Middle Ages, the parish did not aim at forming a community. For the transition to Christianity did not put in question the structures of the social life of the Germans. Through baptism one indeed became a Christian and a citizen of heaven, but this did not involve joining a visible social structure (a church community). One remained in one's previous community, the extended family, the clan, and so on. This grouping as a whole was Christian and that was what guaranteed something like a Christian way of life. So being Christian did not lead to anything like a church community which stood out from existing social ties. The sacramental and cultic acts of Christianity were meant, rather, to hallow the existing social structure and guarantee its ongoing existence.

This status necessarily also led to a change of the role of word and sacraments in Christianity. The communal aspects of the sacrament faded into the background and what came to the fore aimed at the sanctification of the existing community. Thus through the combination of Christianity and early mediaeval society the individual was no longer sociologically speaking a 'citizen' of two 'communities', as in Christian antiquity, but merely in the ontological sense a 'citizen of two worlds', earth and heaven, this world and the next. On earth there was a political community which in terms of traditional religion understood itself as a sacral alliance that absorbed the church community into itself. This social monism of political religion is to be regarded as the metaphysical basis of the proprietary church system of the early Middle Ages and also the sacral dimension of imperial power.

(b) The mediation of grace

With their primitive and archaic religious sense, people found it difficult to cope with the reality of a relationship between human beings and God based on grace, which was difficult to grasp intellectually. They wanted more tangible forms of mediation to which heavenly grace attached itself: in other words, sacred things which were not possessed by demons. The demons were driven out of whatever mediated holiness in the cult by exorcism, and the power of heavenly blessing was called down in benedictions. Exorcism and blessing, performed in sacred rites and with holy words, made these objects holy and sanctifying.

> In so far as there was any transformation here, the understanding can be said to be metabolic rather than symbolic. The object transformed still retained its character of signification (in scholastic terminology this was the relationship between *signum* and *res*, *res et sacramentum*). This understanding is important for what follows.

(i) Mass – priests – communion

This idea of grace had a particular effect on the understanding of the mass. As this had been detached from the context of the church community, transformations, fundamental shifts of accent and new practices were inevitable. In particular it should be stressed that the mass was not a liturgical proclamation which also served the edification of the community, but a cultic event which communicated grace objectively. The focus was on the presence of Christ, often in a physical and reified permanent form. Everything depended on the transformation of bread and wine, and all else in the mass was an extra. People saw the presence of 'sanctifying grace' through the transformation in the mass. So the mass had to be celebrated as often as possible (frequent and daily mass). The mass was celebrated *for* the people, but not *with* the people. For this reason the adoption of Latin and alien cultic language was not a problem. The important thing was not understanding the cult, but its correct performance by the priest.

The priest was understood to be the mediator of grace (*habens potestatem circa corpus Christi reale*, having power relating to the real body of Christ), and this role was emphasized. This led to the priest being given a greater dignity, but it also led to his separation from the laity. However, there was a demotion as well as a promotion. There was not much talk in the Middle Ages of the *potestas circa corpus Christi mysticum* (power relating to the mystical body of Christ). By *corpus Christi mysticum* (or *politicum*) we are to understood the social constitution of the community (or church). In the early church the clergy exercised the functions of governing and guiding the church community. But since in the early Middle Ages the church had largely been absorbed into the political system, the functions of government lay with the noble lords or with the supreme ruler, the king.

In the framework of the metabolic understanding of the sacrament, correct cultic acts were enough. But it looks as if people required from the priest a cultic purity interpreted in ascetical terms. Sometimes this asceticism was rigorous, as with the Donatists, who linked the efficacy of the sacraments with the worthiness of the celebrant. Ascetic rigorism will probably have been a factor in the spread of monastic priests (their ascetic way of life guaranteed that the sacraments they performed brought salvation). At all events, the priest was thought of as being 'more worthy' than the lay person, since only the priest communicated at the mass.

The people communicated only 'at all holy times'. There are different reasons for the awe of communion in the Middle Ages. Probably the rigorous asceticism played a greater role here than the change in the image of Christ (the strict judge, etc., which is often cited as a factor). Account should also be taken of the devotion to relics, which involved veneration and not communion.

Granted, in the course of the thirteenth century there was an extension of the eucharistic cult in the wake of a piety based on the life-of-Jesus piety, but the forms of veneration were governed by the cult of relics. It was all-important that they should be present, and looked at reverently.

(ii) Penitence – confession – indulgences

This topic should be considered against the background of the metabolic understanding of grace and the lack of a community. The early church institution of penance had in fact been a function of the community. In understanding penance in the early Middle Ages we need to begin from the connection between commandment, transgression and atonement. Penance was related with atoning for the deed (= paying the wergild). Paying the price of atonement restored justice and peace. The price of atonement in order to make satisfaction and amend had to be paid precisely (prices for sins were worked out in penitential tariffs). Since doing penance was an objective matter, it could be commuted by the payment of money or simply be performed vicariously.

Mediaeval confession as the sacramental forgiveness of sins in individual confession, which could be repeated at any time, was the result of a long process of transformation in which the public penitential practice of the bishop's church was privatized and extended to the healing of souls, and originally lay 'confession' was clericalized. This combination and transformation took place under pastoral pressures which we can already see beginning in late antiquity. In Christianity with an Irish stamp, which was shaped by monastic asceticism and had no church communities, there seems only to have been private penance. This consisted of confession, the imposition of a penance, and reconciliation (absolution). The granting of absolution was bound up with payment based on a 'penitential tariff'. The juxtaposition of confession and absolution then turned private penance into private confession. In the course of the eleventh and twelfth centuries this process was completed all over the West. Scholasticism then reflected the result in its theology and casuistry.

In the development of indulgences, which became a distinguishing mark of the mediaeval piety of penance and works, first of all we need to note the early mediaeval understanding of penance and secondly the collapse of public penance. According to the 'reformed penitential order' of the Carolingian age, once again reconciliation after certain transgressions was reserved to the bishop. In the case of indulgences, which spread from the middle of the eleventh century, we have the commutation or transformation of imposed penances into corresponding good works. Both commutation and transformation were first intended for penitents who still had to do penance for sins which carried a public punishment, but they were then rapidly extended to all those who wanted to do penance voluntarily. In practical terms the indulgence was a relaxation of penance, but in devotional terms it heightened the penitential disposition. The good works which earned indulgences and were prescribed *in remissionem peccatorum* (for the forgiveness of sins) – participation in crusades, the obligation to study, the performance of particular pastoral tasks, support for church buildings, charitable and social institutions and so on by providing labour or payments of money – might be described as a utilization of the individual potential for penance in favour of the social needs of the time.

The formula *in remissionem peccatorum* was indispensable in connection with meritorious compensation for good works as long as the question of the actual action which forgave sins or the relationship between penance, the repentance of the sinner and priestly absolution was still unclear. Given the scholastic distinction between guilt and the subsequent punishment of a sin (*reatus culpae* or *reatus poenae*) and between eternal and temporal punishment, the indulgence is to be related to the *reatus poenae temporalis* (temporal punishments for sins). Thus eternal punishment and sin are subject to the gracious judgment of God and forgiveness is granted through a combination of sacramental absolution and the repentance of the sinner by virtue of the merits of Jesus Christ. But mediaeval people were not only concerned about the forgiveness of sins; they also feared punishments. They thought of these in quite concrete terms. From the ninth century on there are compelling testimonies to anxiety about both earthly and other-worldly punishments (purgatory). The religion of the time had a great interest in penances which could diminish the *reatus poenae*.

4. The transformation of church order by the feudal system

From the fourth century on, the Roman empire of late antiquity was caught up in a process of transformation which also embraced the church order of the old imperial church and led to the disintegration of the fixed organizational structures of churches headed by bishops. This process to some degree made it easier for the new rulers to accept Christianity and led to its dissemination throughout the proprietary church.

(a) The 'feudal' system

To understand the relationship between the proprietary church and what in due course came to be called the feudal system, we need to go back to the decline of the city in late antiquity. After the rigorous economic and fiscal reforms in the fourth and fifth centuries the Roman empire was increasingly lapsing into archaism, and this led to the decline of the system of government and of city life. In the ancient city all spheres of life had been integrated. The city was the centre of administration (the *curia*), the economy (the *forum*) and religious and cultural life (the *templum*). The surrounding countryside was administered from this centre. As a consequence of the decline in the course of the fifth and sixth centuries a large number of landowners returned to their country estates. They turned them into exempt economic, political and social structures which were self-administered. Because these large-scale land-owners took parts of the *forum*, *curia* and *templum* with them to their estates, they thus became local rulers.

The lapse into archaism in the state and the return to an agricultural economy and administration matched the customs of the new peoples who were streaming into the Roman empire and who from the start had known nothing of city life and state administration. So they accelerated the decline of the governmental system and the city and in the course of the early Middle Ages shaped the whole of life along the lines of what became the feudal system at the expense of the city.

Being lord of a domain involved a complex of private and public rights and can be described as a kind of governmental system in the private sphere. It included rights to the legitimate use of force, administrative responsibilities, the use of the labour and goods of dependents, jurisdiction and police authority.

Thus in its heyday, down to the high Middle Ages, this feudal system can be defined as a comprehensive social and economic order which ruled every sphere of life. Cut off from those with higher authority, members of households and courts lived according to 'court law'. At its heart lay jurisdiction over persons and things.

Jurisdiction over persons (*munt*) covered members of the family proper and persons who were unfree and living in different degrees of dependence. *Munt* was the legal bond between the free and the unfree. The term always denotes a lack of rights, i.e. the dependent relationship of someone in need of protection. The possessor of *munt* gave protection. An existence without *munt* would have been that of a free person. Those persons were free who had an allod, a possession handed down from generation to generation which was worked on by serfs. This possession made them nobles. As the landed ones, they belonged among the powerful, who could help themselves. Without property there was no freedom but only *munt*, which safeguarded the existence of the unfree.

Two things need to be stressed in connection with jurisdiction over things (*gewere*) in connection with the proprietary church. 1. Every object was under the jurisdiction of a person, so as yet there was no idea of a moral person or a person at law. 2. This control aimed not only at protection but also at the use and free disposal of things, and this could involve the lord in trafficking (sale, exchange, pledging and so on).

(b) The proprietary church system

The characteristics of the type of jurisdiction described above also applied to control of the church. The proprietary church can be defined as a place of worship subject to the lord in such a way that he not only had a right to the property and its contents but also had complete spiritual control over it.

The way in which the church was thus at the disposal of the lord was connected with his jurisdiction over things. Since in archaic primitive society every landholding was also understood as a sacral community, a place of worship was needed for the performance of the divine cult. So such a building had to be erected on the lord's land over an altar and had to be provided with the necessary fittings. Since the lord was thought to have full control over everything built on his land, the place of worship was the church of the one who built it. Of course if it was to be regarded as holy, it had to be consecrated. In this way the consecrated object and all that went with it were transferred to God. According to the view of the early church, things consecrated to God were church possessions, which the bishop administered as God's representative. But from the viewpoint of the lord, such a transfer was tantamount to the transfer of the property to the bishop. However, in the proprietary church system the bishop had no control of property. The lord had complete control. Bishops and synods could no more than constantly impress on him the duty of protection and support.

In the economic conditions of the time, such a duty could be fulfilled only if churches which were founded were endowed with land and income. Therefore the Carolingian reform laws in particular aimed at the separation of part of the lord's possessions as 'church property'. However, the legal subject of this separate property was not the church which had been founded or the saint to which it had been dedicated and whose relics were contained in the altar, but the lord, by virtue of being the proprietor. Thus the church which had been founded was very much like a 'firm' in whose name the lord of the church invested part of his property, made use of it, and traded with it. The lord could sell, exchange and pledge his church like anything else; he could make a gift of it, bestow it as a dowry, leave it to his widow or use it for any other form of welfare. What was forbidden was to make any profane use of the church. That churches could be traded did not affect their duty to provide support for the clergy and perform their functions. The only important thing was the profit of the firm.

There were advantages in establishing a proprietary church and transferring property to it. Income could be increased by good management. Moreover, as a possession of the church, property was better protected. Damage by third parties brought down divine punishment. Property was also better protected against being divided up in bequests, and this could contribute towards stabilizing the control of the founder's family. So on the whole it can be said that the foundation of proprietary churches was already among those endowments customary in the Middle Ages which did not cost the founder very much and also brought him material benefit. Of course religious interests also played a considerable role. Founding a church was a pious work which produced treasure in heaven, and the intercession and protection of the saints. Moreover, many early proprietary churches were built over the family tombs of their founders; so the proprietary place of worship became a family tomb and the saint was the heavenly patron of family and court.

Jurisdiction over persons also meant that the lord had full spiritual authority, even over the priest, who became his proprietary priest. A priest consecrated by the bishop was necessary for divine worship in the church. According to the view of the early church, ordination created a legal bond with the bishop. From the perspective of the lord, this would have meant that bishops had jurisdiction over priests. But the clergy appointed to these churches were not released from their obligations to the lord and put under the jurisdiction of the bishop; this dependence on the lord often proved oppressive. To mitigate it, the Carolingian reform legislation of the eighth and ninth centuries insisted on personal freedom and the guarantee of a basic livelihood by the creation of a benefice. Part of the church's income was diverted to provide for the priest appointed.

The priest's personal dependence on the lord and the latter's full spiritual authority were not affected by this. For the lord appointed the clergy, laid down their duties and could dismiss them from service. Since the use of the benefice was transferred with this appointment (investiture), the lord required something in return. He would also take over the estate of a dead incumbent and reserved for himself the use of a vacant position in the interim. Ideas about the lord's jurisdiction over persons and things led to charges for spiritual actions performed by a priest in the lord's proprietary church (stole fees). In this case the spiritual authority of the lord of the proprietary church amounted to the power to excommunicate. The lord commanded his subjects to fulfil their ecclesiastical and religious duties in his place of worship. This compulsory church attendance logically followed from the idea of the dependents of the lord as a sacral community. So in later times it often happened that in places with different lords a separate church was built for each domain.

The lord's power of excommunication and compulsion is to be seen as one of the roots of the mediaeval pressure towards the creation of parishes. All in all, the formation of the mediaeval parish is a complicated process on many levels, and in each instance local conditions need to be taken into account. Intrinsically, pastoral care in the country was part of the bishop's task. But even in late antiquity, pastoral pressure led to some of the centres of pastoral care in the countryside gradually becoming independent. However, at a very early stage these were taken over by local lords and turned into proprietary churches. The introduction of tithes usually accelerated this process of gaining independence from the bishop. For the Carolingian laws stipulated that these offerings which could be exacted from all agricultural produce were to be used to support the pastoral care exercised by the parish churches. It is understandable that the lords were keen to acquire parish rights for their churches, so that they could gain possession of the tithes. The same consideration could also have the opposite result; in order to remain in possession of a large income from tithes, the bishops stopped the development of the country parish system.

Churches could be built only by noblemen who had land. The kings were usually lords of churches on a large scale. However, bishops' churches and monasteries could also act as lords. Where they were not themselves the proprietary monasteries of a king, bishop or nobleman, they too could control proprietary churches.

The links between the proprietary churches and these three main groups meant that in the early Middle Ages church institutions were dependent on different groups. There were the churches under bishops, the churches under the nobility and the monastic churches. Structurally, the task was to end the interlocking and juxtaposition and again bring the different 'churches' into one comprehensive unity.

The early church solution, according to which the bishop's church was to be the point of reference for all other subordinate church institutions, was no longer a possibility. As things were, its place was first taken by the 'king's church' (the church of the realm). In a slow but steady process the king succeeded in incorporating the institutions of the bishop's church, the monastic church and in part also the church of the nobility into his church.

(c) The bishop becomes a lord

The decline of the city which began in late antiquity and which continued into the feudal Middle Ages, transforming all spheres, first led to the dissolution of the bishop's sphere of competence ('the bishop's house')

(i) The decline of the 'bishop's house'

Domus episcopalis, the 'bishop's house', is a legal term for the bishop's sphere of overall competence. He had control over church property;

the clergy were subject to him, and as a rule he paid them. The pastoral care of the countryside belonging to the city was exercised by the church of the bishop in the city. But as the church penetrated into the countryside, the decentralization of pastoral care could no longer be avoided. Centres of pastoral care in villages were granted episcopal rights (services on Sunday and feast days, baptism, penance, etc). Those centres which gained liturgical and pastoral independence can be called 'parishes'. Soon special 'parish' property also came into being, as endowments were given direct to the local churches instead of to the bishop's church in the city. So the episcopal country clergy were the first to be detached from the bishop's house. Of course they had been commissioned for pastoral ministry by the bishop and were dependent on him. So clergy and churches of this kind must initially be distinguished from proprietary churches and their priests.

The separation of the city clergy took place in the course of the early Middle Ages. The decline of the city as a result of the growth of domains ruled by lords was a factor here. It should also be noted that the clergy were constantly active in a large number of churches and chapels in the municipal area of the 'city' in which the bishop resided. The totality of these places of worship in a way formed the 'cathedral', and the clergy active in the individual churches were the bishop's clergy. Slowly, these clergy then became attached to particular churches. Economic independence went along with legal independence through property attached to individual churches which did not belong to the bishop; these developed into monasteries or collegiate chapters.

The 'bishop's house' then completely broke up in the eleventh century. The bishop's clergy, those at his church, which from the ninth century had meanwhile been elevated above others as the main church, banded together as canons and formed the cathedral chapter, a legal and economic corporation which existed alongside the bishop.

The progressive delegation of the pastoral functions of the bishop to other authorities in the course of the early Middle Ages and at the beginning of the high Middle Ages went with the assumption of new functions extending far into the secular realm. This led to the episcopal office becoming more aristocratic. In the course of the development the bishop became lord of the city, lord of the proprietary church and finally the representative of royal rule.

(ii) The bishop as lord of the city

The beginnings of episcopal control of cities are connected with the progressive lapse into archaic conditions and the collapse of government in late antiquity. Because the state offered no protection, the cities had to help themselves. As things were, the bishop, whose administrative role in the community had to some degree still remained intact, and whose church still had considerable resources, was the obvious person to take charge of administration, charitable works and defence. The Lives of bishops at this time praise their activities in this sphere and their concern for the defensive capabilities of the city. In Gaul, the Merovingian kings recognized the bishops as administrators and strengthened their rights and duties as lords of the cities. These ecclesiastical-secular administrative positions had been occupied since the fifth century by members of the indigenous Gallo-Roman land-owning class. As a result of the intermarriage between the indigenous Romanic nobility and the Frankish newcomers, the new aristocratic ruling class also slowly came to occupy the episcopal sees. So imperceptibly the office became increasingly more aristocratic. The episcopal office, thus associated with jurisdicition, was then the prerogative of the nobility throughout the Middle Ages.

(iii) The bishop as lord of the proprietary church

The dissolution of the 'bishop's house' is the starting point for the development of episcopal jurisdiction over the proprietary church. In the course of the Middle Ages the responsibility for things and persons which still pertained to the bishop at various removes were increasingly understood as control of a proprietary church. The bishop became lord of a proprietary church alongside the lay and monastic churches. What in late antiquity was once legally the bishop's church developed into a proprietary church. This transformation was of course a consequence of the omnipresent feudalistic way of thinking. The development was further advanced by confiscations and appropriations.

Charles Martel carried through a confiscation of episcopal church property on a large scale, in favour of the laity. To consolidate his own rule he compelled bishops to hand over portions of church property as fiefs to his followers. He compelled them to make a kind of forced enfeoffment. The Carolingians thus treated episcopal church property as proprietary property, which could also be traded.

In addition to confiscation there was also a form of endowment in which lay church lords handed over their proprietary churches to monasteries and bishops. The Carolingians who became kings status did this in a grand style. For example, in 741 Pepin the Younger endowed the newly founded episcopal church of Würzburg with twenty-four proprietary churches. Such donations gave proprietary churches of kings or the nobility the status of bishops' churches. This confiscation or endowment blurred the rights and responsibilities of the churches in question. The bishop acted as though he were lord over all the churches subject to him and dependent on him, whether these were the episcopal churches which remained after the various divisions, or the proprietary churches which were transferred later. Jurisdiction of persons and things (*munt* and *gewere*) was the governing factor in the control and disposal of individuals and property.

(iv) The bishop as the king's representative

With the bishop as a representative of the king, the development of the episcopate into an aristocracy and its incorporation into the realm was complete. The presuppositions for this process were the way in which bishops had been ruling cities since late antiquity and also the proprietary church understanding of episcopal jurisdiction. What will now be said about the jurisdiction of bishops must be seen in the framework of the Carolingian and German empire which was developing. In particular we should note here the spread of feudalism, whch fundamentally determined the structures of rule.

Feudalism (from *fehu* = cattle and *odal* = possession) is a historical term describing a social order which sums up the many legal relationships of a servant to his master on the basis of mutual loyalty and help. This order underwent fundamental changes during the Middle Ages. The relationship can be reduced to the following scheme. In return for the service of the (free) servant (vassal) the lord (the king or another powerful figure) gives a fief (*feudum, beneficium*) and puts the person thus enfeoffed under qualified legal protection. In the course of its development, the feudalism which decisively shaped the mediaeval state led to social differentiation and a mobility among the aristocracy.

The confiscations of church property by Charles Martel mentioned above were already connected with feudalization; that is even more true of the appropriations by Carolingian, Ottonians and Salians. The reasons for them can be shown from their beginnings among the Carolingians. For his comprehensive reform plans, Charlemagne had given episcopal churches and heads of monasteries far-reaching authority in external administration and internal formation, and for the defence of the realm. The material resources of existing church property were not sufficient for the performance of these functions. Instead of royal or imperial property being given as fiefs to secular bodies as before, bishops and abbots were entrusted with the relevant functions. All the gifts and assignations of public property and rights of sovereignty in this respect served to incorporate the episcopal and monastic church into the state. In the course of this appropriation, some imperial property became state property and some church property became state property. To put it simply, this mixture took place in two stages and in two ways. First royal immunity was granted to existing church property, and consequently the property qualified in this way was endowed with sovereign rights (regalia).

Immunity was a royal privilege through which the territories under episcopal and monastic jurisdiction were removed from the ordinary administration of royal officials and put directly under the king, who had the relevant acts of sovereignty performed by specially appointed officials (stewards). Regalia are to be seen in the first instance as public rights of sovereignty like the collection of tolls, the minting of coinage and forest rights; administrative responsibilities like those of a count or a duke could go with them. Such transferences can be demonstrated from the time of Pepin the Younger onwards. They were carried out on a large scale by Ottonians and Salians.

With the latter, the motives were the same as those of the Carolingians. In each case the church was incorporated into the state, or the aim was a better use of the political and economic resources of the realm to further royal policies. For in the wake of the feudalization of lordship the secular powers treated their royal fiefs and imperial offices as property which they used to develop and extend their own spheres of power. The fief was hereditary and in a kind of 'allodizing', i.e. transference into ownership, was alienated from the realm and withdrawn from both the direct and indirect jurisdiction of the king.

As the process of feudalization could no longer be reversed, the kings had hardly any alternative than first to bind episcopal and monastic church property to the realm by privileges of immunity and finally to confer regalia on bishops and abbots as well. They could do this without needing to be concerned about losing power. For a clergy loyal to the realm and the king had been attracted to the monasteries and cathedral chapters. We need to see the striking promotion of cathedral chapters by the Ottonians and Salians in this connection. The independent corporations with legal and economic independence had to observe the statutes binding on canons, i.e. communal life and celibacy. The king nominated the bishops from this educated and disciplined circle and appointed them to ecclesiastical and royal office by investiture. There was no question of any pressure towards enfeoffment through inheritance here.

In investiture the bishops and abbots were also instituted into the church property of the realm relating to their function. This consisted of old and proprietary episcopal church property and donations by third parties to the church concerned. This mass of property can be compared with the nobleman's allod. However, since immunity had been bestowed on it, it already came close to being property of the realm. That was even more the case with the regalia, which were exclusively the public property of the realm. In reality the differences in origin and purpose became blurred: church property became the property of the realm and the regalia bestowed by the realm became church property.

The fact that it is possible to speak of church property of the realm brings out the link between the church and the king and realm, and the public functions and duties which went with it. The king's jurisdiction over church property of the realm resembled that of the lord of a proprietary church. For in law the king had the supreme dominion; usage was transferred to the bishop or abbot by investiture. The services to be performed by the spiritual office holder were not just of an ecclesiastical and spiritual kind, notably worship; they also included secular functions in the administration and defence of the realm. But the former were also performed on behalf of the realm.

In terms of personal law the incumbents of church property of the realm also worked with the king. That went without saying where the property was in his gift (*munus regale*). However, as this royal office was linked with what was in the gift of the church (*munus sacerdotale*), the bishops were also bound to the king as incumbents of the spiritual office. In investiture, spiritual jurisdiction was also bestowed along with the sovereignty which went with the administration of the realm. The latter related to the liturgical and pastoral tasks in the territory under the church (diocese); the former to the exercise of public authority in a district or a particular sphere of sovereignty.

The king instituted in both areas. The coupling of ecclesiastical and secular tasks made episcopal office a 'royal priesthood'. This royal priesthood matched an idea of jurisdiction which saw the king as also being a priest and bestowed on the 'priestly monarchy' government of the *res publica Christiana* in which the church was distinct from the realm (*regnum*) only by virtue of its functions (cf. II, 2). In sum, the church institutions formed the church of the realm, which because of its bond with the king can also be called the king's church.

4. The jurisdiction of the monasteries

The early mediaeval proprietary church system controlled monastic institutions as proprietary monasteries; as royal abbeys they had been integrated into the church of the realm. In each case the monasteries were given control of property and were drawn into the process of acting as lords. So what has been said about the bishop as lord of the proprietary church and a royal official can equally be said of the head of a propertied monastery.

At the beginning of the development of Western monasticism, the basic formative motive was an ascetic flight from the world: separation from the 'world'. In the view of ascetic monks this also included the bishop's church and its community, which were integrated into public life. The ascetic content of monasticism and its concern to flee from the world must be emphasized. Here was a hostility to the world which was sometimes heightened to become the view that all those who were entangled in 'worldly things' had no chance of attaining eternal salvation. One could understand the ascetical monastic idea as a contrasting model to established society and the aristocratic church of the time. But such a view would overlook the religious and social function of the monastery in the society of late antiquity and the early Middle Ages.

This consisted first of all in vicarious intercession. That was the prime bond between society and monastery. Anxiety about their own salvation and concern for the public good led the nobility of late antiquity and the early Middle Ages to found monasteries. They founded monasteries in which the monks were to pray vicariously for them and to do works of penance. The many foundations of monasteries and individual donations for the purpose of vicarious intercession must also be seen in connection with the decline of the church community. It was the monastery which inherited its function of intercession.

The religious motive of anxiety about salvation was accompanied by the motive of jurisdiction. Monastic service in a proprietary monastery belonging to house and family with its relics and worship served to legitimate rule and bring stability. In this connection, transferring possessions to one's own monastery had an even greater effect than in the case of simple proprietary churches. In this way the ascetic and monastic institution became a cultured monastery, a development which was connected with a growing symbiosis between the nobility and monasticism.

Neither had been possible without a monastic 'turning to the world'. This took place in small steps which initially were barely perceptible. The regulation of monastic life played a prominent part in the development of culture. Thirty monastic rules for Western monasticism have been handed down from the period between 400 and 700. In the course of the early Middle Ages the regulating and disciplining was developed to the point of uniformity. If initially monasticism lived by various rules, at the end of the period the Rule of Benedict was the obligatory norm everywhere. This process of regulation brought discipline and stability into the earlier monasticism, which had been driven by ascetic unrest.

With stability as 'attachment to a place', the first step towards the cultivated monastery had been taken. First of all in the literal sense of the word, the cultivation of the soil; then in the transferred sense as cult and culture, and this led to a slow clericalization and the priestly monk. Ascetic pastoral literature from the past was taken over, so one had to be able to read and write. Soon it was felt necessary to perform functions outside the monastery. First came education and 'pastoral care'. The monastery which became cultivated in this way slowly proved attractive for the nobility as well. With the noble founders and monks, a 'noble life-style' found its way into the ascetic buildings of the monastery. The life-style of the local ruling house came to colour the monastery.

In the course of the early Middle Ages the cultivated monastery took on further tasks in the service of society. These extended into the cultural sphere with the school, into the pastoral sphere with mission, and into the economic and political spheres with colonization and the establishment of rule.

In the Carolingian and even more in the Ottonian and Salian period the link between monastery and monarchy became closer. Monasteries ceased to be proprietary and loosened their local ties, in many cases in order to live under the 'royal protection' of monastic freedom. As abbeys of the realm, monasteries were given royal immunity, and public rights of sovereignty were transferred to them. Like the bishop's church, the monastic church was incorporated into the kingdom, and as a monastery of the realm became an institution of the realm. Endowed with sometimes considerable possessions and extensive public rights, the abbeys of the realm became vehicles of high culture and spirituality.

However dependent or free a monastery may have seemed in individual instances, the proprietary system influenced monastic thought and led to the 'rule of the abbots'. They belonged to the leading class, the nobility. And not only the abbots but also the monks came from the nobility. The royal monastery of the early and high Middle Ages remained closed to the poor of the world.

What has been said of male monasticism is also true of the women's convents. In some instances these were even more aristocratic. For in the aristocratic society of the early and high Middle Ages, entry into a convent was just one possibility for members of the nobility. The convent performed social and pastoral roles for the ruling class. It was thought of as a retirement home for noble ladies, whether these were widows or had remained unmarried. The role played by the convents in emancipation, which can sometimes be demonstrated, was subordinate to this social role. Women went into a convent to distance themselves from the machinations of the crude and warlike world of men.

The function of the convents as welfare institutions also affected their life-style. The *monacha* became the *nonna*. While the term *monacha* (feminine of *monachus*) indicated an ascetic life-style, the *nonna* (venerable matron, grandmother = noble lady) had associations with an aristocratic way of life.

II

The King's Church of the Early
and High Middle Ages

During the early course of the high Middle Ages, under the domination of the papacy, the emergent West gained a new ecclesiastical ecumenicity which led to the *ecclesia urbis* (= the church of the city, i.e. Rome) becoming the norm for the *ecclesia orbis* (= the church of the globe, i.e. Western Christendom). This development was complex and was carried forward (and also hindered) by a variety of forces. For in the decline of the ancient empire not only the political ecumene but also the ecclesiastical ecumene had been lost, since the latter had ultimately been based on the institutions of the empire and the emperor. What persisted of the old church ecumenicity in the Western provinces was a provincialized awareness on the part of the episcopal communities that they belonged together. But their synodical life, which initially was still strong, was taken into the service of the new kingdoms. The autonomous ecclesiastical episcopal synods became councils of the realm under royal leadership.

The Catholic kingdoms of the West Goths, Anglo-Saxons and Franks, who were particularly important for later history, formed what in ecclesiastical terms were regional churches under royal government, that is, where they had not lost any wider cohesion as a result of local proprietary church rule. Only with the formation of wider spheres of jurisdiction and the political ecumenicity which followed did local and provincial churches come to belong together again in a wider union. The power behind their integration derived from the institutions of the Carolingian empire and the emperor. In the abstract we can call this integrating power a 'religious-political principle'. The political ecumenicity shaped by it produced an ecclesiastical ecumenicity, which found institutional expression in the church of the realm.

To this brief sketch of developments we must make one important addition, the bond with Rome. In it were interwoven two notions which in the end led to the identity of the *ecclesia orbis* with the *ecclesia urbis*. One was more connected with the church; the other more with politics.

In considering the church aspect, we need to begin from the ecclesiastical self-understanding of the time. The faith of the church was bound to tradition. Loyalty to it was interpreted as accord with the 'original church', which was seen as the norm for church life.

The West which was being Christianized was shaped by the provincial Christianity of the Roman-Latin tradition, in which despite all the differences there were common features: language, cult, Holy Scripture (the Vulgate), discipline and doctrine. As a result of the cutting off of the Latin churches of North Africa and Spain by Islam, all that was left of the old apostolic churches of the rising West was the Roman church. This deliberately cultivated tradition, and summed up the apostolic tradition for itself as the 'Petrine apostolic principle'. According to this, all the churches on earth had to be in accord with the church of St Peter (cf. below, III, 1, a).

Thus the Roman Petrine tradition became the normative authority as a result of the peculiar early mediaeval situation. The Irish already showed a similar veneration of Rome, which Columba celebrated as 'the most splendid flower of a Europe which has faded, and head of all the churches'. The Anglo-Saxons were even greater admirers of Rome, and in discipline and order modelled their church on Rome. We can call this church a 'regional church tied to Rome'. Boniface was an exponent of the bond with Rome, and he and his Anglo-Saxon fellow-missionaries bequeathed it to the Frankish church. This too became 'a royal church tied to Rome'.

This bond with Rome, which was reinforced by a marked veneration of Peter, must not be imagined as any jurisdictional dependence. It amounted to accord with the Roman church in cult, discipline and doctrine. The head of the Frankish church which in this way had ties with Rome was the king. So as a church of the realm and a royal church it was governed by the political principle.

But ancient Roman traditions entered into this, too. This brings us to a political notion which went with the bond with Rome or the idea of Rome, namely the renewal of empire, a re-establishment of Roman imperial power. First this was thought of in an unclarified mixture of Germanic Frankish ideas and ideas from Roman antiquity, and then at the beginning of the high Middle Ages in terms of a theory of translation which also had a significance for salvation history, according to which Roman rule of the world had passed to the Franks and the German empire. Thus the religious and political ideas of Rome became combined and led to a new political and ecclesiastical ecumenicity in the West, for centuries under the domination of the political principle in religion, the church of the king and the realm.

1. The renewal of empire

The Frankish kingdom created by Clovis was the first large-scale concentration of rule in the early Middle Ages. Granted, the Merovingian kingdom split up into several smaller realms in the course of the sixth century. However, under the Carolingians the concentration of power in one hand began again. Since 680 as 'mayors of the house' they had been able first to develop a local rule in the region of the Maas and the Rhine and finally to become the key power in the kingdom. The victory of Charles Martel over the Saracens at Poitiers in 732 further strengthened the position that had been attained. In the meantime his position had become so unassailable that his son Pepin the Younger (741–68) could venture to depose the last Merovingian king, Childeric III, have himself proclaimed king by the great men of the kingdom in 752 and at the end of the year be crowned king by the Frankish bishops in Soissons.

(a) The alliance between the Franks and the papacy

Rome, too, was on the side of this usurpation. When Pepin enquired whether or not it was good for there to be kings in the realm of the

Franks who had no royal power, Pope Zacharias I indicated that it was better for the real holder of power to be called king than for one to be king without royal authority, so that the natural order was not destroyed. His successor, Pope Stephen II (752–57), again anointed Pepin and his sons at St Denis. This sacral action is to be seen as the seal on the alliance between the papacy and the Frankish realm which was completed with the treaties of Quierzy and Nothion in 754. According to these, the Franks were to protect the pope and the patrimony of Peter against the Langobards and compel them to surrender the territories they had occupied. So the issue was the exempt status of pope and patrimony in Langobard Italy. This highly political alliance, which had important effects, needs some explanation.

As a result of the Langobard invasion of Italy in 568 and the establishment of their rule there, Rome was left only with the exarchate and duchy (the regions around Ravenna and Rome) in Central Italy. Since the Arian Langobards had come over to the Catholic church, a united kingdom of Italy under their rule was a very real prospect. In 751 King Aistulf occupied the exarchate and prepared to occupy the duchy. There was a threat that the Bishop of Rome would be incorporated into a Langobard regional church and thus that the papal claims to jurisdiction over all the church would be thwarted. Byzantium, weakened in political and military terms, could no longer offer any protection. Moreover relations between Rome and Byzantium were burdened with both ecclesiastical and political disputes. However, the Franks could serve as protectors. Charles Martel had rejected papal requests in this direction, but Pepin acceded to them. The title Patricius Romanorum bestowed on him in 754 (probably with the tacit acceptance of Byzantium) obligated him to protect Rome and papal interests. In accordance with the treaties of Quierzy he compelled the Langobards to surrender the exarchate and duchy. But instead of handing these territories back to Byzantium, he gave them into the possession of St Peter. Thus the duchy and exarchate became an autonomous area under papal rule, secured by the Frankish guarantee of support and protection. A papal 'church state' had been created. The background to its creation needs to be illuminated further.

Under the Langobard threat, the Petrine apostolic doctrine which had been shaped in a long tradition and combined with the idea of a Christianized Rome became a piece of political self-help. Here first and foremost it was important to maintain the administrative and ecclesiastical independence which Rome had long since attained through imperial supremacy under Frankish protection and to extend it when times were favourable. The constitutional incorporation into the Byzantine empire was not simply to be abolished with the alliance: it remained fluid until the crowning of Charlemagne as emperor in 800.

> The developed idea of a Petrine apostolic Rome at that time found quite unique and vivid expression in the Donation of Constantine. Scholars have long argued over the place and time of the composition of this document and its intended purpose, and different answers are still given. The majority argue that it was composed in Rome in the second half of the eighth century. There is much to be said for the view that the document is not to be seen as a forgery composed for political purposes but that it is a literary fiction composed on the pattern of late antiquity – a kind of house legend to the greater glory of the Lateran church.

We should reject the view, widespread earlier, that the Donation of Constantine played a role in the negotiations over Pepin's guarantees of protection. For the church state is not the product of a 'refined forgery' but the result of a natural development. Here we should note the autonomous status of the city of Rome within the framework of the Frankish realm, the functions of the popes as rulers of the city, and the application of the economic resources of the patrimony of Peter (= the possessions of the Roman church under private or proprietary law). However, at a very early stage the Donation of Constantine was used as a historical argument for papal claims to territory.

The bond with Rome played a role in the Frankish help for the pope, but so did the political calculation that in this way it would be possible to gain influence in Italy and incorporate the Langobards into the Frankish empire. Charlemagne had himself crowned king of the Langobards in 774. There were sharp reactions after 754 to efforts on the part of Byzantium to regain influence in Central Italy.

Charlemagne's reign (768–814) was marked by considerable expansion and internal consolidation of his realm. Around 800 he extended his rule beyond that part of the European interior which had a Germanic stamp. The symbolic elevation of his rule culminated in his coronation as emperor by Pope Leo II in St Peter's, Rome, on Christmas Day 800. This first Western coronation of an emperor was part of the renewal of the Roman empire.

Ancient Roman ideas were being taken up here, but so too were Frankish notions. First of all the political emancipation of Rome from Byzantium was completed with the proclamation of Charlemagne as Roman emperor, and the constitutional flux over the church state which had existed since 754 was ended. It was put under the protection of imperial rule. However, this rule was not limited to Rome (the church state) but extended to the Roman empire, i.e. to Western Christendom united in the Frankish and Langobard realms. But rule over Europe had fallen to Charlemagne by the grace of God and had not been transferred to him in his coronation by the pope, or even in the proclamation of him as Roman emperor.

Charles certainly made use of ancient Roman traditions, concepts and titles, but his aim was an imperial dignity independent of Roman claims. The Romans did not become the 'people of the empire'. The Franks continued to have that status. The Carolingian heartland between the Maas and the Rhine (Aachen) still continued to be the focal point of the empire. Charlemagne envisaged a Roman empire of the kind existing in East Rome, which had long since detached itself from Rome as the centre of the empire and had achieved independent imperial rule.

In agreements between 831 and 815, Byzantium accepted the claim and recognized Charlemagne's imperial rule as the Western empire. In so doing, Byzantium, despite the title 'emperor of the Romans' which was first introduced at this time, detached itself from the ideal link of its rule with Rome and left the city to the West.

In accordance with the understanding with Byzantium, on 11 September 813 Charles himself crowned his son Louis emperor in Aachen. The model for this coronation was not any papal Roman notion but the Byzantine model. The coronation repeated by Pope

Stephen V in Reims in 816 had no constitutional significance. However, the pope now recalled the Roman papal notion of the origin and function of the name 'emperor'.

The Franks saw the emperor as having the function of preserving the unity of the empire. According to Frankish custom the empire was to remain undivided: i.e., to preserve the ideal of the unity of the realm all the legitimate sons exercised rule. This finally led to the division of the empire into different kingdoms. When the role of emperor was introduced, the unity of the empire could be expressed in a personal rule and the special authority associated with the title could be used in the interest of preserving the empire as a whole. As the imperial dignity largely and expressly served to protect the Roman church, it was only natural to extend the special protection to the institutions of the imperial church and to Christendom as a whole.

Charlemagne's court created lively propaganda for a renewal of Christian empire, taking up biblical imagery, even before Charlemagne was crowned emperor. Here the emphasis was on the sacral dignity of his rule and a renewal of the empire in administration, culture and religion.

These efforts found expression in extensive legislation enacted by imperial councils. This attacked the excesses of the proprietary church system, helped to extend pastoral work in the countryside, and aimed at the unification of law and administration. Considerable efforts were also made to raise the cultural level through educational reforms.

Scholars have spoken of these efforts as a 'Carolingian Renaissance'. At that time the foundations were laid for a uniform Western culture of educated men. Here the efforts at unification and a bond with Rome are striking. Thus for example a uniform script (Carolingian minuscule) was developed which replaced the previous multiplicity of special local scripts. Latin was corrected along patristic lines and developed into the uniform language of mediaeval culture. In the pastoral and liturgical spheres there were lively exchanges between local Gallo-Frankish liturgies and Roman liturgies to form a uniform liturgy of the Latin West. The great variety in monastic life-styles was to be unified with the Rule of Benedict. Norms for clergy, who exercised their ministry together in churches, also aimed at discipline and uniformity. In all this the model of the early church could be detected. People saw Rome as having preserved its tradition. Individual knowledge was extended in a lively collection of canons.

So political renewal stood in a reciprocal relationship with church renewal and the renewal of religious culture, and all in all led to a recognition of the Petrine apostolic principle. However, this was only an ideal, and as yet it did not entail any jurisdiction.

(b) The renewal of empire in crisis

Charlemagne's empire was still unfinished. Louis the Pious (814–40) had the difficult task of continuing and completing the renewal that had been begun. However, he did not get beyond making a beginning. With the rebellion of his sons (833), a decline and disintegration set in which could not be stopped. The empire harboured too many social, political and ethnic differences to be capable of long-term survival. Moreover the technical and administrative means which the agricultural economy had at its disposal were not enough to hold the disparate structure together.

Despite all the attempts at constitutional ordinances about succession and the relationship between kingdoms and empire, like the *Ordinatio imperii* (817), the process of the regionalization and the independence of kingdoms could no longer be halted. Despite all the vows of 'brotherly harmony' there was a dispute among the heirs. Clients and local power groups gathered around the rival Carolingians. In the course of the ninth century there were concentrations of power all over the landscape and changing groups of alliances. But a new political order began to emerge, despite all the instability in relations. Rule came to be stabilized in limited areas stamped by historical tradition. In these small areas of pre-national statehood, the efforts of the Carolingian renaissance were taken further.

Rome in particular was affected by the disintegration of the Carolingian empire in the ninth century. For Italy, like the West Frankish kingdom, was caught up in an increasing regionalization of rule which sometimes made Rome the focus of rivalries.

Under the strong rule of Lothair I and Louis II as kings of Italy

(817–55 and 855–75), which went largely unchallenged, the popes were concerned to support the kingdom and respect its sovereignty over the church state. The Roman constitution (824) had emphasized this much more strongly than the *Pactum Ludovicianum* of 817. With this imperial privilege Louis the Pious had granted the pope autonomy for the church state and freedom in 'papal elections', contenting himself with a mere recommendation. However, the relative autonomy now drew the papacy into the rivalries between the nobility of the city of Rome and the nobility of central and Southern Italy, behind which Byzantium was often to be found, seeking to regain influence in Italy. To avoid the dangers which arose from this, the Roman constitution put more emphasis on the sovereignty of the empire; the emperor also claimed a say in papal elections and required an oath of loyalty from the Romans. The defeat of Louis II by the Count of Benevento in 871 shook the Carolingian position in Italy severely. Central and Southern Italy in particular became the battlefield over power and influence.

These bloodiest of power struggles which drew the papacy in out of sympathy have gone down in history as the 'dark century'. In it popes were blinded, mutilated and murdered. At one synod in 896 even the corpse of Pope Formosus was exhumed, displayed and desecrated.

The chaos into which Rome had lapsed was reflected in the cruel events which usually went with a rapid change of popes. The papacy became the plaything of the feuding nobility of the city of Rome and central Italy. Popes were deposed and appointed depending on the political situation. Here local and wider interests and conceptions clashed. One trend can be called the 'foreign party' and the other the 'local patriots'. The former sought links with the empire or parts of it, in the Carolingian imperial tradition (the renewal of empire). This policy, which also had ecclesiastical motives, had, for example, persuaded Pope Formosus (891–896) to crown Arnulf of Carinthia, king of the East Franks, emperor in 895 and to drop the exponent of local forces whom he had crowned shortly beforehand, under pressure. After the surprise departure of Arnulf, the opposing party took bloody revenge on Formosus and his followers.

With Arnulf's death in 899 the Carolingian involvement in Italy came to an end. The 'foreign party' now followed the Italian kings who dominated the scene in rapid succession. In the local party the family of the older Tusculans succeeded in establishing themselves. From 901 they dominated Rome and the church state and survived all attempts to overthrow them. Alberic II governed the church state with a strong hand from 928 to 954 as a regional ruler who was completely independent. During his principate the popes were his creatures and were restricted to activity within the church. He repudiated any kind of renewal of empire by refusing imperial coronation.

The limitation to Rome and the church state brought stability and order to the region, as it did to other pre-national territories, and this had a positive influence on church life. Under Alberic II the monks of the city of Rome also established links with Cluny.

The weak point of Tusculan household policy was its neglect of the Petrine apostolic principle. The Tusculans would also have found it difficult to base their rule on Petrine apostolic notions. So they attempted to revive the splendour of ancient Rome. However, a renewal of empire limited to the city and taking up pagan antiquity had now become obsolete. Rome's past had long had a Christian stamp. Here too the early mediaeval bond with Rome had held through all the decline of the Carolingian empire. The pious veneration for St Peter and his successors had not ceased.

The German empire combined the political and religious ideas of Rome. The East Franks, too, had not been spared division into petty kingdoms. In the dispute between the Carolingian heirs, the delegated mandate holders from the nobility had gained their independence in the process of feudalization. The dukes (*duces*) in particular had succeeded in bringing together old historical areas with a degree of ethnic homogeneity as tribal duchies (Bavaria, Swabia, Saxony and Franconia).

However, under the influence of the Carolingian royal tradition they did not decide for total independence but for a federal alliance in one kingdom. After the death of the Carolingian Arnulf of Carinthia, they did separate from the Carolingians with Louis the Child (900–11) and Conrad I (911–18), but with the election of Henry I, Count of Saxony (919–36), as king they continued the notion of unity, which found legal and institutional expression in the term *regnum Teutonicorum* (German empire). Under Henry's son

Otto (936–73), structures were consolidated and royal power in the empire was heightened. Deliberately based on the Carolingian model, Otto's real accession to the throne took place in Aachen Cathedral, in a coronation ceremony. The act of coronation then remained a model for all the Middle Ages. As a counterbalance to the counts, royal vassals and unreliable kinsfolk intent on independence, in a continuation of the Carolingian tradition the king relied on the episcopal and monastic institutions and integrated them into his church system. By his victory over the Hungarians at Lechfeld near Augsburg in 955, Otto proved himself *imperator*, a true military ruler, increasing the empire by his eastward-looking policy and by regaining Lombardy.

The opposition to King Berengarius brought him to the region in 950. On 15 December 950 Otto was crowned king of the Lombards at Pavia. At that time a journey to Rome for an imperial coronation had probably already been planned. However, Alberic II still barred the way to a renewal of empire by Otto's coronation as Roman emperor. It was his son Octavian, as Pope John XII again combining the spiritual and secular rule of the church state in one hand, who in a period of oppression called for Otto's help and crowned him emperor on 2 February 962. After the long period of autonomy for the kingdom of Italy, Rome and the renewal of empire were again linked.

So we have to say that the strengthened German monarchy snatched Rome from its self-limitation and again gave it ecumenical breadth. The Ottonian renewal of empire restored the city and gave it an appropriate place in the structure of the empire.

(c) The Ottonian and Salian renewal of empire

The coronation on 2 February 962 followed the model of Charlemagne's renewal of empire. But the legal character of the coronation had meanwhile changed. In the dispute between Charlemagne's heirs over power and precedence within the corporate Carolingian rule, coronation by the pope in Rome had come to be recognized as being the decisive factor and was no longer regarded as subsequent confirmation and blessing. This had been the issue in the papal coronations of Louis the Pious and Lothair I, on whom their imperial fathers had previously bestowed the title of emperor (in 813 and 816 respectively).

An equally important shift in function was also bound up with this change. The office of emperor was primarily associated with the protection of Rome and the church state. Aspects of this idea already found expression in the construction of the coronation liturgy. A later time had only to clarify the thinking a bit further to interpret the imperial dignity as church office: protection of the church of the city of Rome and the universal church on behalf of the pope. The candidate to be elected by the pope or the crowned emperor could thus be examined to see if he was worthy of office.

That was not as yet the issue in the coronation of the Ottonians and Salians in the tenth and eleventh centuries. The German kings alone did the 'electing'. Nor were they the ones who were examined to see if they were worthy of office; the popes were. For in the renewal, pope and church state were again incorporated into the empire. Granted, in the imperial privilege of Otto the Great, the Ottonianum, issued after the coronation and made more precise after the deposing of John XII (963), the autonomy and protection of the church state were guaranteed, but so too was an imperial say in the election of the pope, and the pope was required to make an oath of loyalty to the emperor.

As we saw, the 'imperial people' of the empire were the Germans, not the Romans. It is hard to discover or specify the precise nature of the link between *regnum* (kingly power) and *imperium* (imperial power). The reinforcement of the sacral status of the king over against the powerful princes of the realm and a deeper legitimation of the imperial church system must also have been factors. Moreover, the renewal of empire was increasingly no longer understood in the way it was in the time of Charlemagne. The reviving empire was to be the continuation of the old Roman empire, in other words not just half an empire alongside that of East Rome, but the imperial power which had been handed down from the Romans (East Rome) through the Franks to the Germans (the translation theory). However, such a notion would have had no basis without any link with the city of Rome.

At least Emperor Otto III (996–1002) tried to put this political theory into practice. He envisaged a Christianized ancient empire with Rome as the imperial residence. In 996 he appointed a relative, Gregory V (Bruno of Carinthia), as pope over the bewildered Romans. After Gregory's death he had his teacher elected pope. Gerbert of Aurillac called himself Silvester II (993–1003). The name amounted to a programme and fitted the new Constantine's idea of renewal.

As emperor he not only renewed the letters of protection created by his ancestors for the Roman church; in his own power he bestowed lands and rights to rule on St Peter and his representative Silvester. According to this the church state owed its existence to imperial donation. Otto III saw himself as lord of the church and at the same time as its most humble and loyal defender. Recognition of the greater honour, the spiritual pre-eminence, of the church in whose service he believed himself to be was also expressed in devotion and zeal.

The brilliant emperor who pursued such utopian ideas died suddenly at the age of twenty-two. The German princes united round the Count of Bavaria, who was elected and consecrated king in Mainz as Henry II (1002–24). He returned to the Realpolitik of Otto the Great and based the renewal of empire on his position in the German kingdom, which he attempted to reinforce by the consistent completion of the church system. He associated the sacral view of the monarchy and its function in the *sacrum imperium* with the spiritual and religious concerns of Cluny and other centres of reform. The Salian Henry III (1039–56), who is to be seen as the representative of an idea of a renewal of empire ultimately to be understood in theocratic terms, in which papal Christian Rome played such a significant role, was full of ideas about the renewal of empire through reform in the spirit of the time. Conrad II (1024–39) had also expressed this idea in titles and had written in the inscription round his imperial seal: '*Roma caput mundi, tenet frena orbis rotundi*' (Rome, the head of the world, holds the reins of the wheel of the world). Henry III no longer called himself *rex Teutonicorum* but *rex Romanorum*, thus announcing the claim of the Germans, as the people of the empire, to the imperial throne. In this way they also had increased responsibility for Rome, the spiritual centre of the *sacrum imperium*, which for Henry III was a renewal of the Roman church in the reforming spirit of the time.

In Rome the renewed incorporation of city and church state into the empire had met not only with assent but also with rejection. Time and again there were revolts by the 'local patriots'. After a period of relative quiet under the younger Tusculan popes who were loyal to the emperor (1012–44), there was again confusion in Rome. In Silvester III another pope was set up against the pope of this family, Benedict IX. Granted, he was driven out again and soon seems to have renounced his papal claims. But Benedict IX had also been compelled to resign in favour of a kinsman (Gregory VI). However, this had not made things any clearer. Henry III felt compelled to intervene. At the Synod of Sutri on 20 and 23 December 1046 he sat in judgment on the popes and deposed all three by virtue of his own authority. The new pope whom he designated was Bishop Suitbert of Bamberg, a member of the imperial episcopate, who called himself Clement II (1046–47). He crowned Henry emperor on Christmas Day 1046. The subsequent popes who were designated by the emperor were also members of the imperial episcopate: Damasus II (1047–48), Leo IX (1048–54) and Victor II (1055–57). Henry did not simply want to incorporate Rome into the imperial church as a proprietary church but to establish a close bond between the papacy and the empire.

The massive interventions in the church of the city of Rome and the designation of 'foreigners' as popes are to be understood as an expression of the religious and political renewal of empire, in which the issue was the interplay of *regnum* (kingly power) and *sacerdotium* (priestly power) under the jurisdiction of the emperor. This responsibility for the church of Rome was recognized and celebrated even before the first 'Gregorian reformers'. But after Henry's death the model of renewal under the powerful and protective hand of the emperor suffered a crisis. It collapsed, and made room for new ideas about the freedom of the church.

2. The relationship between secular and spiritual power in the early and high Middle Ages

The topic amounts to a history of political theory at this time. It needs at least to be sketched out because the power of kings from Charlemagne to Henry III was also of decisive significance for the church. This power prescribed the status and function of papal authority in the state.

(a) The power of the king

During the period that we are to consider, the power of kings was predominantly in the structural and legal sphere. Christendom consisted of as many units as there were more or less autonomous kingdoms. The rulers, i.e. kings and emperors, fitted the different church institutions together to form a royal church or a church of the realm. The ruler had a sacral dignity. Three elements above all supported the sacral notion of the ruler: political religion, the theory of proprietary churches, and the idea of the king.

We can sum up the content of political religion briefly in the statement: all religion is public and all that is public is religious. For *res publica* and religion belonged together. This unity needs to be emphasized. A division into two fundamentally different (or even only separate) spheres was simply unimaginable.

It must be noted and emphasized that in proprietary church theory all rulers understood themselves in sacral terms. The lord was responsible for the sacred by virtue of his jurisdiction over both persons and things (*munt* and *gewere*). And what can be said of the lordship at a local level (cf. above I, 4) also applies in the case of royal rule on a wider scale.

Proprietary church theory and political religion were introduced into the idea of the monarchy. The early mediaeval monarchy developed in the course of the settlement of the various Germanic tribes and the system of rule which came into being on the territory of the ancient Roman empire. Constitutionally, the development of the new form of kingdom must be seen as an important result of a fusion of ideas about rule deriving from the Germanic tribes and from the Rome of late antiquity. However, the new institution was fragile in various respects and exposed to rivalry. Success, above all success in battle, was required of anyone who was to be acknowledged king.

Kings were constantly confronted with the right of the nobility to resist. This was not affected by the ideological elevation of the royal family on the basis of hallowed blood, i.e. its alleged descent from the gods or a heroic ancestor. The myth of blood could not be Christianized. The notion of priesthood offered a substitute: royal unction and consecration, i.e. consecration as king based on Old Testament models. In the Frankish kingdom the unction and consecration of Pepin in 752 were the model. In the ninth century the coronation liturgy was developed and the king's sacral dignity emphasized. The longing for stable rule in the midst of political rivalries under the Carolingian heirs was crucial to this sacralization. The bishops, who in the meantime had been important decision-makers in politics, had an interest in a strong monarchy.

The coronation of a king involved more than blessing and intercession for the member of a royal family or the nobility who was elevated to be king in the presence of the great men of the realm. It was seen as a sacramental act which brought about what it denoted. So the consecration became an essential element in the exercise of rule. The one who was consecrated was exalted to a priestly and sacral sphere. Alcuin taught Charlemagne that he had to govern and direct the city of God built up at the cost of Christ's blood, and that the universal church was sustained through his rule. The bishops celebrated their king with hymns at the imperial council of Frankfurt in 794: he was lord and father, king and priest, the ruler by grace of all Christians. Here was an elevation and election of the one who had been consecrated and crowned. *A deo coronatus, a deo electus* (crowned by God, elected by God) was the tenor of the coronation liturgy. The divine vocation and commissioning was reflected in the titles kings bore subsequent to the Carolingians: *divina favente clementia; miseratione divina; gratia dei rex Francorum*, etc., all denoting divine favour.

Priestly and royal dignity were also symbolized by the different signs of rule. The imperial crown, which was probably made for the coronation of Otto the Great, has to be seen as an outstanding monument to the mediaeval idea of the king and ruler. The full symbolic programme probably came into being in the St Alban Monastery in Mainz. The key saying which often recurs in form and decoration is a quotation from Isaiah: Jerusalem, you will be a fair crown in the hand of the Lord (Isa.62.3).

(b) The status of the king in the church

The different notions of the time about the relationship between papal authority and royal power, and especially about the status and function of the king in the church and in Christendom, can be derived from two theories which in practice amount to the same thing: the king as the visible head of the church. One theory can be called theocratic monism, the other theocratic dualism.

(i) Theocratic monism

In the monistic theory the priesthood is clearly subordinate to the monarchy. The king is the ruler of the Christian state. The so-called Anonymous of York attests to the monism of power.

Under this name are collected a series of treatises which were written around the year 1100; their author has never been discovered (though he may well have come from northern France). The Anonymous begins his reflection on the relationship between *sacerdotium* and *regnum* with christology. The all-embracing characteristic of Christ is his rule of the world, which is superior to his priesthood (= the redemption). This priority is not only temporal but also holds in the order of being. Rule is grounded in the eternal Godhead. This is what makes the redemption of the world possible, in that humanity is taken up into the divinity of Christ. The being of the eternal king is the presupposition for the being of Christ as priest. The world, i.e. human beings, forms Christendom, and this is identical with the church. It is the body of Christ, and Christ is its head; but Christ is not the head as redeemer but as king. So the church under Christ as king is called *regina*, queen, and not, say, *sacerdotissa*, priestess.

The political consequences which the author of the treatise draws from his theology of Christ the King should be clear. The earthly king is the image and representative of Christ. The earthly and visible church is entrusted to him. The king appears as Christ's representative on earth. The priest cannot be such a representative. For as priest Christ had no kind of lordly power. Therefore the priesthood which continues the function of Christ the priest also has no kind of authority to rule. The priesthood is called to sanctification and redemption. The governance of the church lies in the hands of the king. This makes the world the reflection of the heavenly city.

The assignations of the functions of *sacerdotium* and *regnum* in the Anonymous can be repeated and made more precise with terminology which only developed later: the priesthood has *potestas circa corpus Christi reale* (power relating to the real body of Christ) in an exclusive and distinctive way; the monarchy has *potestas circa corpus Christi mysticum* (power relating to the mystical body of Christ, see p.16 above). 'Mystical body' must be understood as the visible and social structure of Christianity. The shaping of this in the power and government of the church is part of the king's function. *Potestas circa corpus Christi reale* is understood in the narrow sense as the power to turn bread and wine into the body and blood of Christ; in a wider sense this can be extended to any priestly mediation of salvation. That is reserved to the priesthood. Moreover the Anonymous puts considerable emphasis on the honour of the priesthood, just as on the other hand he sharply rejects all papal claims to rule of the church.

Of course the Anonymous is not yet thinking of a purely spiritual church separated from a temporal church. The church institutions are those of the king, and the bishops are the king's privileged dignitaries. He has in mind the 'royal priesthood' of his time. So in practice there is hardly any differnce here from the theory of theocratic dualism.

(ii) Theocratic dualism

To clarify this, we may take a propaganda document of Henry IV from the year 1076, which is a justification of the deposing of Gregory VII (see III, 1, c). The main charge against him is a failure to observe God's ordinance, because he has arrogated to himself secular and spiritual power:

'Thus he has failed to observe God's gracious ordinance, which wills for this to be founded not on one but in principle on two powers, namely worldly and spiritual, to which the Redeemer himself referred during his passion, when he said that the two swords, which are at the same time symbols, are sufficient. When it was said to him, "Lord, here are two swords", he replied "it is enough", and by saying that these two swords were enough he was indicating that a spiritual and a worldly sword are to be wielded in the church. With them, all that is harmful is to be cut out: he teaches that every man should be compelled by the spiritual sword to obey the king who rules in God's place, while the secular royal sword is waged externally to drive away the enemies of Christ, but internally to compel obedience to the spiritual power. And so it should be drawn in love by one against the other, the worldly power not being deprived of respect by the spiritual power nor the spiritual power being deprived of respect by the worldly power.'

Accordingly, the church in its concrete form is identical with the Roman empire (= the body of Christendom). Law and order (peace) are created in this visible structure of the rule of Christ through royal power and papal authority. Both authorities have the same origin (they are appointed by God) and aim (the shaping of the body of Christendom). They are divided in respect of their different functions. The harmony of the world according to God's plan for salvation depends on a right combination of the two tasks. Here the monarchy is to defend and extend faith, the priesthood to hallow and reconcile. In so far as the institutions of the priesthood are integrated into the realm as the king's church, the king also governs the external affairs and interests of the priesthood: the conveyance of the material basis for the spiritual tasks of the clergy; nomination and investiture of church officials.

As functional dualism, this model of order emphasizes the special competence of papal authority and attempts to do justice to it. However, by its theocratic elevation of the monarchy which also has the external means of power at its disposal, the theocratic dualism ends up as a monism. In disputes the competence of the competence lies with the monarchy.

There are a large number of texts presenting a theocratic dualism from the Carolingian period on. Despite all the variations in image and concept the direction remains the same: the priesthood has been entrusted with the keys of the kingdom of heaven, the monarchy with the sword for punishing evil. In the latter relationship the *sacerdotium* is under the *regnum*; in the former the relationship is reversed. In the latter case the king is 'son', in the former he is the governor of the church.

Both concepts finally led to the construction of the imperial church, which was imitated in a different form in the small-scale structures of pre-national statehood. Because royal authority had a sacral character, the priesthood could also participate in the royal power. It was not thought of as contradictory to their spiritual office that bishops or abbots should be chancellors, court officials, diplomats and generals.

3. *The culture of the king's church*

After the Christianization of the Roman empire the cult and religious life of the episcopal churches were also at the service of the public. In the early Middle Ages and at the beginning of the high Middle Ages this function was brought out even more. Apart from the various church institutions there were no longer any other vehicles of culture. The empire and the kingdoms of the time took account of this situation and put the material means for cultural work at the church's disposal. The patronage of the rulers was exclusively for its benefit.

Cathedral foundations, monasteries and royal court chapels were the vehicles of cultural life and spiritual activities. The beginnings of the Carolingian renewal were continued and deepened. So scholars also speak of an Ottonian renaissance, in which formal education in the framework of the seven liberal arts reached a noteworthy aesthetic level. This benefited historiography, liturgical texts, hagiography and biblical exposition in particular. There was not yet the power for original speculation in philosophy and theology. On the other hand, there were outstanding achievements in the illumination of books, architecture and sacred art. A detailed description would amount to an account of the history of Romanesque art.

Sociologically, Romanesque art and culture were aristocratic. Those who promoted it and gave commissions belonged to the nobility and reflected the understanding of the world among the nobility and rulers. The splendour, pomp and value of artistic objects great and small and of literary works convey a view of the splendour of power as a reflection of the splendour of Christ, power (the power of rulers) as participation in the power of Christ. So this culture was shaped by secular commissions and secular concerns. The political virtues of justice and the keeping of the peace shaped the portraits of the rulers of the time, as it did the hagiographical glorification of the saintly nobility as founders of churches and monasteries, as defenders of the realm, as fathers of the fatherland.

The harmony of *regnum* and *sacerdotium* in the culture of the church of king and nobility also included harmony between the powerful and the poor, social harmony. 'Class distinctions' were not put in question but interpreted as an expression of divine order. But the powerful were constantly reminded of their duty to those who had no protection. Considerable attention was paid in the models for rulers of the time to the welfare of the poor.

However, to live with the poor and like the poor was not an ideal for the piety of the time, either for the worldly nobility or for bishops, abbots and clergy. It was not even an ideal for the monks, who since ancient times had been called 'Christ's poor'. They were to be advocates for the poor. Thus many social and charitable tasks were transferred to the monastery. The monks prodded the consciences of the powerful, not to protest against the system but to confirm it, asking for help for the unprotected and helpless, for the sake of the salvation of their souls.

On the whole, the literature of the time gives a picture of a harmonous combination of power and powerlessness, of poverty and riches. It is beyond the capacity of historical judgment to answer the question whether this harmony was the expression of a universal accord, since the evidence that has come down to us is that of members of the ruling class. However, it is certain that this harmony no longer commanded general assent after the middle of the eleventh century. On the one hand it had been shaken by a popular movement from below, and on the other it had been devalued by that trend in the priesthood which saw the church of the noble rulers no longer as a reflection but as a perversion of the divine world order. This period also saw a crisis of ruling monasticism and new reflection on its roots in an ascetical escape from the world.

III

The Papal Church of the
High Middle Ages

In the course of the twelfth century the institutions of the aristocratic, monastic and episcopal churches came together to form a corporation under papal leadership. So the political principle was replaced or at least suppressed by the Petrine apostolic principle. Given this process, we can speak of the mediaeval papal church, just as for the previous period we can speak of the church of the realm or the king's church.

The conviction of the precedence and superiority of the *sacerdotium* over the *regnum* and of the 'freedom of the church' led to this momentous detachment of the church from the *sacrum imperium* and its transformation into an independent corporation.

The Gregorian reform developed the principles for this and formulated the inflammatory slogans which first found an echo and assent in widespread religious asceticism. Moreover in the intellectual blossoming which can be detected after the end of the eleventh century the scholars then took up the cause of the reformers' 'freedom of the church'. That was especially true of the canon lawyers, who set to work giving the church a new structure from top to bottom.

The *Concordantia discordantium canonum* created by Gratian around 1140 (the Decree of Gratian) is a landmark in the development of the science of church law: commentators on the Decree are known as decretists (twelfth century) and commentators on the papal decretals (published from the end of the twelfth century and by Gregory IX) as decretalists.

Challenged by this task, in their science of canon law they worked with that rational spirit which became a general characteristic in the course of the twelfth century and fascinated the intellectual elite of the West. Thus the canon lawyers formed a guild of scholars who were particularly associated with the papal church. With their professional knowledge, they had a competence which commanded the broadest assent. Of course the 'freedom of the church' argued for on the basis of the Petrine apostolic principle was focussed not just on the papal claim to leadership within the church, but also on an authority to intervene deep into the secular realm. What the sacral kingship had done for religion and culture, for the defence and extension of the faith, was from then on to be defined as the function of the papacy, and its execution was to be delegated to the relevant authority.

These papal activities, extending well into the secular sphere, must be seen against the background of the political situation in the West. There was no longer a comprehensive *sacrum imperium* in the twelfth and thirteenth centuries. Since the Gregorian reform its splendour had faded: ecclesiastically and spiritually as well as politically and socially. The restoration of the *sacrum imperium* by the Hohenstaufens in the second half of the twelfth century no longer worked in the face of the new political, social and cultural tendencies of the time. The city states of northern Italy and the various kingdoms of Europe, beginning with those of England and France, were rivalling the German empire in power and no longer allowed Europe to have an 'age of the Hohenstaufens'.

The papacy encouraged this political division of Western Christendom into different kingdoms and derived benefit from it. It emphasized the plurality of secular powers and the unity of spiritual power. As long as the different secular powers as *regna* had not yet matured into the statehood of the late Middle Ages, they recognized the spiritual authority which culminated in the pope. The spiritual *imperium* of the mediaeval papal church in the twelfth and thirteenth centuries was to this degree the consequence of an underdeveloped statehood in the individual kingdoms; it was also the expression of a general Western culture which was unthinkable without Petrine apostolic Rome. The West, at the beginning of a slow ethnic and political differentiation, could no longer tolerate any political ecumene, and instead recognized and furthered the legal, cultural and religious ecumenicity recognized and promoted by the papacy. In this condition of underdeveloped statehood the model of the attribution of *sacerdotium* and *regnum* developed from the Petrine apostolic principle seemed to be more convincing in theory and more useful in practice than the competences of the sacral emperorship derived from the political principle in religion.

1. The Gregorian reform

The term 'Gregorian reform' is used by historians to cover the period at the end of the eleventh and beginning of the twelfth centuries which was full of new religious and ecclesiastical ideas and shaken by church political struggles. It must be called reform, in that religious concern for the church culminated in the vision of a 'freedom of the church' through which the order previously dominated by the proprietary church system and the king's church was to undergo a fundamental transformation. With its emphasis on the special character of the church and the clerical status of its offices, the movement for the freedom of the church raised fundamental questions about the relationship between church and world, spirit and power, poverty and riches, and thus released energies which led to a new definition of the relationship between *sacerdotium* and *regnum*. The papal church of the high Middle Ages is unthinkable without this new conception of the church and Western Christendom.

The development of new aims is called the 'Gregorian reform' after Pope Gregory VII (1073–85), who is to be regarded as its special exponent. From the pontificate of Leo IX, which is taken to mark the beginning of the new orientation on reform, as the monk Hildebrand the later pope played a leading role in the circle of reformers who had gathered in the Roman Curia. Other prominent figures were the Italian Peter Damian from the eremitical movement and Humbert de Silva Candida, who came from Lothringia and was deeply influenced by Cluny.

The initial intention was probably, as a result of the death of Emperor Henry III, not only to consolidate reform in Rome but also to make the papacy generally its advocate. The substance of the reform was a moral renewal in an ascetic and monastic spirit, combined with a clarification of the legal and theological positions of the Roman church in Christendom. Humbert de Silva Candida introduced a shift towards criticism of the system when in his polemical writings he began a fundamental rejection of the proprietary church system and the king's church. Gregory VII shared this standpoint. The 'freedom of the church' was combined with the leadership of the church by the pope and this was proclaimed as the task of reform.

(a) The programme for the 'freedom of the church'

We can see the call for the 'freedom of the church' as the slogan for the concerns of the Gregorian reform. The programme of freedom was developed from the theological conception of the church, the work of God on earth founded by Christ. Christ did not entrust the church to kings but to priests. The link between Christ (bridegroom) and church (bride) continued in the bishops and came about through church investiture, in which the betrothal was depicted by the ring and the task of spiritual guidance by the staff. The spiritual character of church office was thus emphasized and investiture was declared an act of the church. Here was a verdict on the proprietary church system and the church of king and empire. The government of the church by the monarchy was presumptuous and a perversion of the divine order, casting the church into servitude and robbing it of its freedom, even hindering its task of bringing salvation. For the sake of salvation the servitude had to be ended and its due freedom had to be restored to the church. Nicolaism and simony were seen as the direct expression of this servitude.

The battle against nicolaism took up the demand for the celibacy of the clergy in connection with Revelation 2.6. This was seen as a consequence of the image of the church. For the relationship between Christ and the church in the image of bride and bridegroom also applied to the individual priest. The community entrusted to the priest was regarded as his bride, whom he had to serve fully and completely.

The Reformers saw simony as the fundamental evil of the time and the roots of the sinful perversion of God's order. The name and concept of simony are intrinsically old and derive from the attempt by Simon Magus to purchase spiritual office for money as related in Acts 8.18. But the old heresy of simony was now extended to the appointment of the clergy to church office by the laity. 'Lay investiture' generally was branded as simony. The statement 'that in no case shall clergy accept church positions from laity, whether for money or for any other consideration', was constantly quoted as a demand at the reform synods.

The leading ideas of the 'freedom of the church' were disseminated in an extensive literature and some of them were passionately discussed. The synods played an important role in the formulation and dissemination of the demands and claims of the reformers. For in the course of the Gregorian reform there was a considerable reactivation of synodical life along the lines of the early church.

In general these synods can be said to have been 'church' gatherings. The particular synods often also had papal legates as members, and were directed by these legates. The Lateran synods were the most important. These were assemblies of the clergy of Rome and the Roman church province which by old tradition were held at the beginning of Lent. But now they lost their local colouring. There was a concern to speak for the whole church. Bishops from abroad often took part in them.

> The Lateran synods held under the presidency of the pope marked an important step towards the mediaeval papal councils in which the convening and direction of a council by the pope or the reception of its decisions by him made it an ecumenical council. In this sense the synods which were later elevated to the status of 'general councils' were papal councils: the First Lateran Council (1123); the Second Lateran Council (1139); the Third Lateran Council (1179); the Fourth Lateran Council (1215); the First Council of Lyons (1245); the Second Council of Lyons (1274); the Council of Vienne (1314).

The Roman Lateran synods in the second half of the eleventh century received papal decrees and also shaped the reform proposals into synodical canons. These were directed above all against nicolaism, simony and lay investiture. Free election of bishops and canonical investiture was called for. But on the whole those making these demands were content to make them as a matter of principle and passed over matters of detail. So the specific details of free election and the legal steps towards canonical institution to office had not yet been fixed. It was the canon lawyers of the eleventh century who first ordered and regulated the procedure. In the first flourishing of the Gregorian reform there was rapid agreement on what was no longer wanted: the nomination of church officials by the laity and lay investiture. How a 'free election' was imagined is demonstrated by the decree for the election of a pope promulgated at the Lateran synod on 13 April 1059.

What should be noted in this document, which also sheds light on how the cardinals saw themselves, are its occasion and purpose, its content and significance. The decree was occasioned by the election of Nicholas II in December 1058, which offended against tradition. After the death of Stephen IX (29 March 1058), those groups of the nobility which were not content with the direction of the reform sought the election of the Tusculan Benedict. The supporters of reform did not recognize him, moved to Siena and elected Archbishop Gerhard of Florence pope. The decree took up the process of election in Siena and legitimated it, making the following regulations. 1. The cardinals exclusively have to elect the pope: here the cardinal bishops have the initiative in nominating candidates; the cardinal priests and deacons propose the candidates; clergy and people have to assent to the vote by acclamation. 2. Rome is the place of election provided for by law. But even an election made outside the city for compelling reasons remains valid if at least some of the clergy and people assent to the election. 3. After election and acclamation the person elected enters office. The liturgical and legal acts of enthronement in different churches in the city of Rome are not part of the 'installation of the pope'. They are part of the liturgical ceremonial, but in exceptional circumstances can be omitted. 4. The papacy is understood as an institution of the whole church and not just of the city of Rome. For this reason the pope is elected by the cardinals as representative of the whole church. 5. Under the influence of this notion the laity are excluded from the process of election. The limitation of the circle of electors is directly aimed at the nobility of the city of Rome, but it is also indirectly aimed at the emperor. For the right of the German king to have a say, which was safeguarded in old treaties, is passed over silently.

Because of the special occasion, we must be careful not to attach too much importance to this decree. It was not followed literally in the subsequent period. Nor were the details of the process of election sufficiently precise for its implementation. However, the electoral decree gave a sign which also remained a guideline for the future: the laity no longer have any direct say in the 'free election' of the pope. The cardinals became established as the real and legitimate electorate. In Siena the supporters of the reform enacted a model statute which made some impression. Both the Roman nobility and the German king had to become resigned to it.

(b) The papal claim to jurisdiction

The 'freedom of the church' was bound up with the Petrine apostolic principle. This was not an invention of the period but was simply developed further at the time. The Gregorian reformers summed up the theory, which had been developed in a long tradition, and first of all tried out its practical applicability at a favourable juncture. A systematic doctrine of papal primacy of jurisdiction within the church with authority to issue directives which also covered the wordly sphere was formed only during the course of the twelfth and thirteenth centuries.

The fundamental notions about the papacy in late antiquity after the fourth century are important for the historical development of the Petrine apostolic principle. They were based on passages about Peter in the Bible, the foundation of the church of Rome by Peter and the apostolic authority associated with it, and the special position of Rome in the empire. The formulations of Petrine claims need to be considered in the context of the rivalries between the patriarchates (especially the rivalry between Rome and Constantinople) and the concern to achieve church autonomy in the face of the theocratic rule of the emperor, which absorbed any special status. Even in late antiquity, the claims led to reflection on the two powers of the pope which were given classical expression by Pope Gelasius I in the twin terms *auctoritas sacrata pontificum* and *potestas regalis* and had a lasting influence throughout the Middle Ages. Note should be taken of the bond with Rome which existed in the early Middle Ages and the permanence of the church institutions of the city of Rome, which was combined with relative political autonomy. In the general transformation, the church of the city of Rome more than elsewhere preserved the episcopal constitution of the early church into the Middle Ages and thus formed something like the core of the episcopal church alongside the monastic church and the church of the nobility. Despite the temporary limitations Rome imposed on itself, the notion of the renewal of empire should also be connected with this.

Despite all the disintegration of the episcopal churches as a result of the proprietary church system and their incorporation into the king's church, the knowledge of spiritual church autonomy and independence had not been completely suppressed elsewhere in the early Middle Ages. The Pseudo-Isidorian Decretals are notable evidence of this.

In the strict sense of the term these are a collection of papal letters (or extracts from papal letters) and council decisions from between the end of the first and the beginning of the eighth centuries in the West Frankish kingdom. The author of the collection called himself Isidore Mercator and in the Middle Ages was identified with Isidore of Seville (died 636). In the wider sense Isidore (Pseudo-Isidore) also stands as an eponym for three further collections which were made at the same time and in the same area: the *Collectio Hispano-Gallica*, the *Capitula Angilramni* and the collection of *Canons of Benedictus Levita*. Since the nineteenth century, all four collections have been lumped together under the heading Pseudo-Isidorian Decretals (or Pseudo-Isidorian forgeries).

The authors all use the same method. They collect decrees, edicts and letters and arrange the material systematically. In the process texts are also freely invented, and authentic material is torn from its original context and used in a different one. This gives rise to alterations of meaning and deliberate falsifications which are used in the service of a special concern: in accordance with the model of the early church, episcopal authority, which in the present is enslaved by proprietary lords, kings and the metropolitans allied with them, must be restored. The papacy is regarded as the guarantor of this episcopal freedom of the church. For this reason there is massive emphasis on the Petrine apostolic authority of the Roman church.

The Pseudo-Isidorian decretals were disseminated as a handy reference work and written out in new collections. On the whole only what conformed with prevailing customs was accepted. For the most part, the Petrine apostolic statements were passed over. Even in Rome, the collection was fully received only in the second half of the eleventh century and integrated into the Roman papal vision of freedom.

One prominent document of this Petrine apostolic ecclesiology is the *Dictatus Papae*, consisting of twenty-seven statements, which Gregory VII had compiled, probably at the beginning of his pontificate. The statements 1. emphasize the position of the Roman church in the church universal; 2. draw conclusions for the authority of the pope as universal leader; and 3. specify the privileges of the pope as the head of the *sacerdotium* over against *regnum* and *imperium*.

The main notion is the honour of the Roman church and the papacy. 'The Roman church was founded by God alone.' This fundamental statement in the first sentence should be noted and understood as a conclusion from the Petrine apostolic interpretation of history. As mother of all other churches, the Roman church must pre-eminently have the characteristics of the whole church. Rome is therefore the stronghold of the true faith, from which it has never departed (Sentence 22: 'The Roman church has never erred, nor, as witness Scripture, will it ever do so'). For his task of guiding the universal church the pope has a special holiness of office and cannot be deposed (Sentence 23: 'That the Bishop of Rome, if he has been canonically ordained, is undoubtedly sanctified by the merits of St Peter, on the testimony of St Ennodius, Bishop of Pavia, with the support of many fathers – as it says in the decrees of the blessed Pope Symmachus', and

Sentence 19: 'That he must not be judged by anyone'). The sentences about the leadership of the whole church are concerned with universal legislation, jurisdiction and comprehensive authority to rule, i.e. a power of jurisdiction which extends to the whole church. Sentence 26 ('That no one may be regarded as a catholic if he is not in agreement with the Roman church') combines dogmatic and legal competence. Here we have the Petrine apostolic reinterpretation of the apostolic principle of the early church, *ubi episcopus, ibi ecclesiae* (where the bishop is, there is the church). As this is developed, a statement from the episcopal ecclesiology of the early church, *extra ecclesiam nulla salus* (there is no salvation outside the church), is also included. The ecclesiological concept presupposes the autonomy of the *sacerdotium* over against the *regnum*, and the subordination of the latter to the *sacerdotium*. The rights reserved from this for the pope are listed in the following sentences: 8. That he alone may use the imperial insignia; 9. That the pope is the only man whose feet shall be kissed by all princes; 12. That he may depose emperors; 27. That the pope can absolve subjects of the wicked from their fealty to them.

A vigorous dispute broke out over the tradition, occasion and purpose of the *Dictatus Papae*. For a long time the sentences were seen predominantly from the perspective of the controversy between *sacerdotium* and *imperium* and interpreted as programmatic theses and a battle programme. Here the much more important ecclesiological aspect fell into the background. Scholarly 'Old Catholicism' saw (and still sees) the *Dictatus Papae* as a breach of church order. However, if the sentences are seen only as headings for a collection of canons, as the widespread 'index theory' suggests, the wording of individual sentences is relativized. In that case they must be interpreted on the basis of similar sentences in earlier and contemporary collections of laws, and above all the letters of Gregory, most of which have been preserved. Even if the index hypothesis is insufficient explanation of the origin of the sentences, and they had the character of programmatic theses, their peculiar literary genre would have to be noted. Its significance only becomes evident in a comparison with papal practice and the broad literary tradition of the Petrine apostolic principle.

From this perspective the charge of a breach of church order also loses its weight. The *Dictatus Papae* can certainly be said to break with proprietary churches and the king's church. The bishops of the imperial church allied with Henry IV of course accused Gregory VII of this. In so doing they referred to the tradition, i.e. to the distribution of competences in the imperial church. But in still basing themselves on the early church here they missed the point even more than the papal ecclesiology did. For early church order had been transformed in the course of the early Middle Ages and the beginning of the high Middle Ages.

The Gregorian ecclesiology had also been shaped by these transformations. It saw itself as reform and played off the truth of the early church against the custom of the king's church. But this creative reference was made in the conditions of the time, and the vision of the 'freedom of the church' was decisively shaped by the positions which were being fought against. On both sides the issue was on what principles the formation and structure of the church, its unity, visibility and order, were to be based. From the Middle Ages onwards, the task posed to the those in positions of power and leadership was to bring law and order to Western Christendom. Where the adversaries had a stature which set them above local situations, they were agreed on this historical duty. The conviction and hope that spread in the course of the second half of the eleventh century was that according to the divine plan of salvation this task belonged to the *sacerdotium* and not to the *regnum*; nor was it a special opinion limited to the Roman reformers. Bernold of St Blaise (who died in 1100) gave expression to the widespread view with the emphatic confession: 'I venerate the Roman see like Christ's judgment seat; its decisions like a sanctuary of the holy Spirit. I regard the pope's decrees as the edicts of the heavenly court' (*De damnatione schismaticorum*).

(c) The investiture dispute

The occasion for the fundamental clashes between *sacerdotium* and *regnum* which deeply shook the basic and hitherto 'hallowed order' was provided by a variety of episcopal nominations in the imperial church. Unlike his father, Henry IV (who had been regent since 1065) failed to combine spiritual and religious considerations with his political interests. Gregory refused to recognize the appointments, admonished the king and threatened him with excommunication. Thereupon at a synod in Worms on 24 January 1076 Henry had the papacy of Gregory VII declared invalid by a majority of his bishops. In a sentence in the form of a prayer addressed to St Peter, the pope excommunicated Henry on 22 February 1076 and released all subjects from their oath of fealty. The dispute over the nominations of bishops had become a matter of principle, which rapidly took on a political dimension.

In the empire an opposition group of rulers formed which proved dangerous to the king. In this difficult situation the king decided on penance in order to deprive the opposition of the semblance of legality. At the castle of Canossa in Northern Italy on 28 January 1077 Gregory absolved the king and received him back into communion.

In the eyes of contemporaries the famous and much mis-interpreted journey to Canossa was not a humiliating imposition on a ruler. By public penance Henry was able to show himself before all the world to be a just king. At all events, as a penitent he got the better of the politician in the pope and compelled him as a priest to accept the penance and remove the excommunication. The pope was probably interested only in demonstrating the precedence of the *sacerdotium* and he hoped for an understanding with the king. However, here he was thoroughly disillusioned. For the lifting of the excommunication once again gave the king ground to stand on. After his victory over the princely opposition with which Gregory was still allied and a second excommunication, Henry regained strength for a counter-blow. At a synod in Brixen in 1080 he had Gregory deposed again. An imperial pope was nominated in the person of Archbishop Wibert of Ravenna. As Clement III he crowned Henry IV emperor in Rome on 31 March 1084. Gregory had previously fled from the city and had sought the protection of the Normans. He died at Salerno on 25 May 1085.

The emperor seemed to have won all along the line, and sacral kingship and the right of kings to invest bishops seemed once again to have been restored. But the reform circles did not bow to this course of affairs. Slowly they recovered their capacity for action. The imperial pope was not recognized. On 24 May 1086 after long negotiations the reform cardinals agreed on a successor and chose Abbot Desiderius of Monte Cassino as pope. However, there were disputes over the line to be followed, and these proved difficult to resolve. It was only on 21 March 1087 that Desiderius had himself crowned pope as Victor III. He died as early as 16 September of the same year. After laborious negotiations on 12 March 1088, the cardinals agreed on Cardinal Bishop Odo of Ostia as the new pope. In Urban II (1088–99) the Gregorian reform had again found a leader who was generally recognized in the Christian West. The imperial pope faded out of the picture almost completely. His fate depended on that of the emperor, who in the vicissitudes of the investiture dispute, which had degenerated into mere politics, was ultimately compelled to resign by his own son (Henry V).

However, there was no agreement on the investiture question even under Pope Paschal II (1099–1118). Certainly the agreements between Henry V and him in the treaty of Sutri (9 February 1111) provided for a radical solution: the emperor was to renounce spiritual investiture and the bishops of the empire the royal regalia. This radical solution came to grief on the solid resistance of the bishops concerned and the nobility of the empire, whom in the circumstances the emperor had not really taken seriously. Thereupon Henry V exacted the old investiture rights and had himself crowned emperor by the pope on 13 April 1111.

These violent events caused sheer indignation among the reformers, who in the meantime had established a strong position which met with widespread acceptance, and diminished respect for the emperor. In the long run Henry's unyielding line in the disputed question of investiture could no longer be maintained. However, there were negotiations only under Pope Callistus II (1119–24). The former Archbishop of Vienna was one of the reformers. But he combined firm principles with adaptability over particular issues. This skilful politician and diplomat succeeded in reaching an agreement. This was sealed in the *Pactum Calixtinum* of 23 September 1122 in Worms and confirmed by both the Bamberg Reichstag (1122) and the First Lateran Council.

According to this agreement the German king granted the 'free election' of bishops and renounced investiture to spiritual office with ring and staff. The bestowal of regalia took place with secular symbols and was regarded as a secular act. In the German empire the king received them before the spiritual investiture, but in the kingdoms of Italy and Burgundy only afterwards. With the concession of the complete independence of the church state from the empire this papal structure of rule was guaranteed the 'freedom of the church'.

By comparison with the original vision of freedom, this was a modest result. For while the spiritual office was 'liberated' from the king in the Concordat of Worms, the church property which continued to be linked with the regalia was not. A freedom of the church which went any further was impossible in the power structure and social structure of the empire. Only a compromise could be achieved, as in England (1107) and France (1098). In neither land was the bestowal of regalia on bishops the rule, just as the connection between episcopate and monarchy was not as advanced here as in the German empire. The investiture problem affected royal power far less than in Germany. A solution was easier to find in England and France.

In both these countries the kings renounced nomination and investiture. So account was taken of the principle of the Gregorian reform that no church office can be bestowed and transferred by a lay person, and thus the spiritual character of church office was emphasized. With the recognition of free election and investiture as a sacramental act of the church only one aspect of church freedom had been resolved. For here too church property was connected with a variety of public duties and both its existence and use were safeguarded by royal protection. So church property was guaranteed by worldly rule. Thus it was as it were the connecting link which again bound the monarchy to a church which had become free in the investiture dispute. In an act of sovereignty called a concession the king bestowed the temporal rule connected with the spiritual office on a bishop or abbot and in return required an oath of loyalty and various services.

2. Political and social effects of the 'freedom of the church'

The assent which the reform papacy 'free of the emperor' had found in the West with Urban II may be taken as an indication that the programme of the 'freedom of the church' under papal leadership matched the ideas of the time and brought all hopes together as it were in one slogan. But that does not mean that those who broadly assented always and in each case held the same views as the champions of the Petrine apostolic principle. Rather, other religious, political and social concerns were associated with the leading views of the reformers. Through this amalgam of different interests and motives and also of diffuse aims reform initially gained a power with which it succeeded in invading the fixed system of the imperial church and the *sacrum imperium*. But these different thrusts also introduced a development which went far beyond the Gregorian reform.

(a) The strengthening of political particularism

The beginnings of the Gregorian reform took place in a context which favoured its supporters. The regency for the emperor's son Henry IV (1056–65), who was not yet of age, did damage to the position of the king in the empire which could not immediately be remedied. The particularistic forces made contact and developed their independence. Local rulers again became independent, especially in imperial Italy. The Reform papacy found effective political support in the Margravate of Tuscany both against pressure from the city of Rome and against Henry IV. The same was true of the Normans of southern Italy, who evaded imperial supremacy in 1059 by receiving their kingdom as a fief from the pope.

All in all it can be said that the particularistic forces of Europe and the empire were not among the allies of the emperor. For as things were, the 'freedom of the church' called for by the Gregorian Reform primarily affected the *imperium Romanum*. Granted, the position of the 'emperor of the Romans', i.e. the German king, was not established in Western Christendom, and there could be no question of an imperial supremacy over kingdoms that did not belong to the empire. However, the weakening of the emperor's position to which the ban on investiture necessarily led was not inopportune for the reformers. That was even more true for the princely opposition in the empire. Without royal investiture the imperial church could no longer be regarded as support for the king. The bond between king and episcopate could be broken and new alliances could be forged between the local nobility and the episcopate. In areas of the empire shaken by civil wars during the investiture dispute the beginnings of such a development were already becoming evident.

Here we should note the different effect of the resolution of the investiture dispute on England and France from that on the German empire. Here, despite the emphasis on the spiritual character of church office, the king's church was strengthened. For the bishops and abbots saw the monarchy that was developing as a guardian of the freedom of the church, whereas the local feudal powers were oppressors. The Gregorian reform led to an alliance of the monarchy with the episcopate against the local nobility. In the course of the alliance, episcopal cathedrals which had often become dependent as particular churches now became as it were royal cathedrals.

By contrast, in the German empire, where in the course of the tenth century the episcopal and monastic churches had been more successful in escaping the influence of local rulers and were subject to the king as churches of the realm, as a result of the alliance of papacy and nobility the Gregorian reform led to a weakening of the imperial church. The investiture dispute benefited the aristocracy of the empire and in the long term led to a consolidation of the territorial forces which were developing.

The imperial church was also drawn into the process of an initial territorialization. For the Concordat of Worms elucidated relations between the church and the empire and between the bishops and the king. As ecclesiastical officers the bishops were bound to the pope as head of the Roman church, and to the king only as the proprietor of the regalia. As imperial fiefs the regalia given to the bishops were affected by feudalization, i.e. by the movement towards independence. The sphere of jurisdiction of the royal regalia slowly became a territory of the empire and the imperial bishop became a spiritual territorial ruler. The secularizing pressures of this effect can be demonstrated from the history of episcopal and abbatial rule of territories from the end of the investiture dispute.

In imperial Italy the empire had a new opponent alongside the feudal forces, namely in the cities, whose economic strength was developing. They began to oppose the rule exercised by the bishops of the imperial aristocracy. The political struggle for autonomy was connected in Milan and other Lombard cities with the social and religious concerns of a lay movement, the Patarines. Their agitators passionately opposed the secularized church dominated by the nobility. Their concerns and demands found recognition and support in the reform papacy.

(b) Church reform and ascetic rigorism

The Patarines of northern Italy were simply an offshoot of a religious revival movement which had been spreading since the middle of the eleventh century. The reasons for their rise have to be sought partly in the growing social and economic differences in Western society, and partly in a deeper appropriation of the Christian tradition. In these revivalist circles, which were also invaded by the lower classes, the harmony between the powerful and the poor, the church and the nobility, lost plausibility, and the culture of the aristocratic church with its splendour and brilliance was put in question.

The unrest and uncertainty was nourished by a rural biblicism and an ascetic rigorism in which Manichaean influences from the East can be detected. Nearer to home were the dualistic views which had always been an undercurrent in monastic asceticism and which could be fed by traditional monastic and patristic edifying literature. Neither the old bishop's church in its pastoral instruction nor ancient monasticism had come to terms positively with power, rule, possessions, art and education. The Gospels made only negative comments on these things. So the ascetic reinterpretation of the Bible was enough to provoke criticism of aristocratic culture and the church.

At this point the social and religious movement joined forces with the Gregorian reform, in which in any case asceticism was held in high esteem. The members of the popular social and religious movement who attacked the crimes of the great and decried the churches of the prelates as cattle stalls may also have been the ones who called for a boycott against married priests and 'simonists'. Thus the Augsburg annals of the year 1076 report: 'The monstrous decree on the continence of priests is being disseminated by laity . . . The priests are wretchedly being driven from the church because of their marriages and the purchase of church posts.' A 'Neo-Donatism', of which Humbert of Silva Candida was also a supporter, was spreading, connecting the effectiveness of the sacraments with the sanctity of those who administered them. The rigorists understood holiness in ascetic terms. Whereas in the first half of the eleventh century ascetic rigorists who goaded people to excesses against the clergy and rulers were regarded as heretics and executed, in some circumstances the agitators now found support from the papacy and the Gregorian reformers. For example, when a priest Ramihrdus had been burned as a heretic in Flanders in 1077 because he had declared sacraments dispensed by simonists to be invalid, Gregory VII condemned the judges to be punished.

So in a way the 'heretical protest' against the church of the nobility became an ally of Gregorian reform. Given this alliance, we are justified in saying that in the second half of the eleventh century there was no longer any heresy in Western Christendom, since in its attack on simony and the royal church the papacy itself had become heretical and was able to draw in all its opponents with the call for the 'freedom of the church'.

With the compromise of Worms, which continued the imperial church and thus the secular power of bishops, and explicitly gave the pope independent rule in the church state, the link between reform and ascetic rigorism was loosened. From the middle of the twelfth century, parts of the religious and ascetical movement turned to the idea of the 'pure church'. In association with the Cathars it thus became not just anti-clerical but largely also anti-church (cf. below IV 3, b, ii).

Arnold of Brescia (who was burnt as a heretic in 1155) can be regarded as a prominent exponent of the reaction which was developing. This educated man who came from the movement of the canons was not yet a Cathar, but fought the clergy and above all the papacy, who were defending their possessions. The papacy, he believed, had falsely turned the freedom of the church into the freedom of the church state, which it defended with force and war against the political freedom of the communal city movement. This warlike priesthood was to be avoided, because it was seeking to establish the church of God with blood. Arnold found followers among the communal movement of the city of Rome, whose predecessors, the Patarines in the cities of northern Italy at the end of the eleventh century, had still been on the side of Gregorian 'freedom of the church'.

(c) Church reform and monastic freedom

There was a close connection between contemporary monasticism and the Gregorian reform. Here special mention should be made of Cluny and the reform monasticism which was seeking to introduce new forms of life and expression. Scholars have different views of the significance and influence of Cluny on the Gregorian reform, but what is beyond dispute is the far-reaching moral and spiritual influence of Cluniac monasticism in the course of the eleventh century and the pro-Gregorian attitude of Cluny in the controversies of the investiture dispute. But Cluny was neither a propagandist of the reformers' freedom of the churches, nor did it inspire it. For both ecclesiastically and socially, the culture of this monastic centre had developed within the old system, and it also had friendly relations with the Ottonians and Salians.

In Burgundy, outside the empire and therefore without the effective royal protection enjoyed by the imperial abbeys, Cluny fought for monastic freedom against the control of the monasteries by the nobility and the bishops. This was its achievement in the history of monasticism and its special position in the tenth and eleventh centuries. The renunciation of control and his proprietary rights by its founder, Count William of Aquitaine, marked the beginning of Cluny (910). Distinguished abbots who ruled for a long time succeeded in building up the great and widespread association of Cluniac monasteries, which enjoyed the widest monastic freedom, guaranteed by the papal protection which Cluny had enjoyed since its foundation. The designation of the abbot by his predecessors and self-investiture were the legal characteristics of the freedom and independence of this monastic church.

In self-investiture the abbot designate took up the symbols of his abbatial rule, which had been left lying on the high altar; instead of being instituted to office by the king or the local ruler, he as it were took up the office himself.

But this freedom was not an alternative and contrasting programme to the imperial monasticism of the royal abbeys, nor did it have any direct connection with the reformers' freedom of the church.

Only with the transfer of the Cluniac model to reform monasticism in the empire were monastic freedom and papal protection combined with the freedom of the church. This took place in the course of the second half of the eleventh century, thus leading to hostility to the royal and imperial churches. Monasteries were founded which appealed to papal protection and the freedom of the church and were in no way subject to the king. The free election of the abbot and the guardian (who was the legal advocate of the monastery and protected its secular interests) was called for, and the demand was zealously supported by those members of the nobility who founded monasteries. Instead of granting the king rights of protection and influence over the monasteries which they had founded, they handed these over to the pope and gave the monasteries freedom to elect abbot and guardian. At the same time they managed to make their pious foundations serve their own interests in another way. Above all in northern Germany, numerous monasteries of Benedictine reform monasticism were created which combined monastic freedom with the Gregorian freedom of the church. Supported by the powerful local nobility which was opposed to the monarchy, these monasteries – like Hirsau – proved important supporters of the Gregorian reform.

The canonical movement was closely associated with the Gregorian reform. Ascetic discipline for the clergy on the model of the early church (cf. Acts 4.32) and the 'statutes of the fathers' were among the demands of the Gregorian reform and led to the formation of communities which from the beginning of the twelfth century went by the rule of St Augustine. These rapidly spread through Europe in numerous monasteries and smaller associations as canons living under the rule.

In this respect they differed from the canons who continued to live after the *Statuta canonicorum* of 816 and did not observe the stricter rule imposed by the new statutes. Because they went by the Rule of Augustine the new canons were called Augustinian (Austin) Canons. They also included the Premonstratensians, who developed from an ascetic community of itinerant preachers led by St Norbert of Xantia (1145) into a canonical order.

Their monastic freedom committed them, like reformed Benedictine monasticism, to the Gregorian freedom of the church.

Different ascetic and monastic groups at the end of the eleventh and beginning of the twelfth centuries who were distinctive because of their eremitical flight from the world were supporters of radical freedom. Their concern for freedom ultimately had ascetic and monastic roots. Liberated from the social and cultural pressures of the monastic institutions like Cluny and the imperial monasticism which had been integrated into society, they wanted to be 'free for God'. For the sake of this goal these reform groups rejected the various services which the monasteries performed for society, renounced greater possessions and retreated into uninhabited areas. The widespread eremitical movement of the time was wholly stamped by this ideal, as were the beginnings of the Cistercians, the Premonstratensians and the various communities of canons.

Cîteaux was founded by Robert of Molesmes in 1098: with the appearance of Bernard of Clairvaux in 1113 the primary abbeys spread rapidly by the filiation system (La Ferté, 1113; Pontigny, 1114; Clairvaux, 1115; Morimond, 1115). The individual monasteries were bound together as the Cistercian order by visitations and a general chapter.

This movement found support and protection from the papacy of the Gregorian reform and took its side.

Thus in a variety of ways the religious and monastic asceticism of the time allied itself with the concerns of the Gregorian reform, which as a result of this alliance gained a moral force that is difficult to overestimate. The rise and rapid dissemination of lay brothers in the reform monasteries is also connected with this important link between the freedom of the church and monastic ascetic ideals. There was a progressive 'monasticization' of the secular servants of a monastery which resulted in the acceptance of lay people as part of the monastic community.

3. The papacy: the ideal and the political reality

The 'freedom of the church' which Gregory VII and his supporters had envisaged was in some respects a utopian and unreal vision. The limits of the freedom which could be achieved for the church became evident in the compromise with which the investiture dispute was settled. However, all in all the papacy emerged strengthened from the dispute. Its claim to rule within the church remained undisputed, and even the precedence of the *sacerdotium* over the *regnum* was at least recognized in principle, where in the event this was not to the detriment of the interests of the *regnum*.

(a) Institutional consolidation and recognition

The first striking thing about the papacy is the consistency of the institution, as demonstrated by the unbroken succession of pontificates. This continuity was shaken only by two schisms, and only in the second half of the thirteenth century did the institution find itself in a paralysing crisis which showed itself in long vacancies in the see.

Such consistency is to be seen as a result of the rapid rise and development of the Curia, which became an efficient body with which the secular kingdoms of the time had nothing to compare. An account of the details of its development, especially that of the chancery, belongs elsewhere. Equally important is the social history of the top levels of curial administration, in which group interests were concerned to secure a seamless administration, and, where there were conflicts, sought to neutralize them.

The college of cardinals became established at the head of the curial authorities as the real decision-making body. It understood itself as an extension of the pope and collegially took part in all the important decision-making processes and decisions of the Curia. The popes of the time were largely just the exponents of the group in the college which was setting the tone. Since the cardinals formed an oligarchy, one can only speak of papal monarchy with some qualifications, and there is no question of there having been unlimited papal rule. Even the popes had to secure majorities for their policies.

Given the pending decisions of often great religious and ecclesiastical significance and of even more church-political significance, it was inevitable that trends and parties would develop within the college of cardinals. Family, local and political interests were coupled here with religious and spiritual ideas and options in church politics in ways which historians can no longer elucidate.

So the 'freedom of the church' which was secured at the beginning of the twelfth century did not simply do away with the 'secular' interest. The pressures of circumstances and the need to make decisions which, given the different interests, led to different options, were not simply channelled through an institution and were balanced out in the college of cardinals and in papal elections.

The dissent over the nature of the further course of reform which had been deepening since the pontificate of Callistus II (1119–24) ended with a double election. Whereas the 'old Gregorians' wanted to see the continuation of a more militant and uncompromising ascetic and monastic line, the 'young Gregorians' argued for compromise with the kingdoms and the bishops. The ascetic and monastic impulse towards reform was to be introduced into the existing hierarchical institutions and transformed for the needs and tasks of episcopate and clergy.

In an irregular election the younger reform group (which was still in a minority) proclaimed Innocent II (1130–43) pope, while the conservative majority party elected Anacletus II (1130–38). Formally, the election of Anacletus was the more correct. However, in the long run Innocent II prevailed, finding support from the reform orders (Bernard of Clairvaux), the famous teachers of the schools of France and the majority of the kings of the West. With the death of Anacletus on 25 January 1138 the schism came to an end.

Whereas conflicts over reform within the church had led to the schism of 1030–38, the schism of 1159-81 was over politics. Frederick Barbarossa (1152–90) pursued with energy and consistency the consolidation of his influence in imperial Italy and followed an Ottonian-Salian model in his relations with the priesthood. It seemed advisable to a minority in the college of cardinals not to respond to this new challenge with a confrontation. After the death of Hadrian IV (1154–59) they elected Victor IV pope (1159–64). The 'anti-Hohenstaufen' majority party had elected Alexander III (1159–81). In the peace of Venice (1177) the emperor recognized Alexander III and dropped the imperial pope Callistus III (1168–78) who was then reigning. The trend supported by the theological schools and monasteries of Western Europe and by widespread public opinion celebrated Alexander in the schism as the 'poor pope' who was persecuted by imperial power, an attitude which also had overtones of disgruntlement with Teutonic power. This support, to which was added the political support of the Italian city states which were fighting for their autonomy and that of the kings of England and France, who in a variety of alliances were seeking their own advantage, ultimately compelled the emperor to fall into line.

With Alexander III, who had previously been a celebrated canon lawyer, the generation of academically trained canon lawyers came into their own in the Curia and elsewhere in the ecclesiastical and religious life of the time. In short, we can say that the popes elected by both the old and the young Gregorians were visionaries, and those from the second half of the twelfth century were practical politicians. The former still lived by monastic asceticism and monastic theology, the spiritual content of which Bernard of Clairvaux had presented so urgently to the Cistercian pope Eugenius III (1145–53) as the guideline for action. Contemplation of eternal salvation was to give power and content to political action. The popes who had been influenced by legal learning began from the fullness of power bestowed by God and from that derived legal claims which, however, they sought to adjust to what was politically practicable.

The outstanding figure among the 'lawyer popes', indeed the outstanding figure of the whole epoch, was Innocent III (1198–1216). At the age of thirty-seven the highly gifted Lothar Segni, with a theological and legal training, was elected pope as being the most capable member of the college of cardinals. Innocent turned the reformed Curia into an excellent instrument for his own use. He consolidated papal rule in the church state by the recovery of territories and rights which it had lost; this was important, since it served as a political and economic basis that gave the popes of the twelfth and thirteenth centuries room for political manoeuvre. As head of the *sacerdotium* and thus as the representative of the spiritual unity of Western Christendom, Innocent sought to achieve a balance of forces and a balance of interests among the different kingdoms of Europe and thus secure a peaceful order all over Europe. He was also recognized as a kind of universal arbiter. In an unprecedented way Innocent summed up the ecclesiastical and political claims deriving from the Petrine apostolic principle in decretals, and thus systematized them, though in political reality this system could only be handed down in an adapted and more developed form. His lofty approach inspired by idealism made it easy for him to find a hearing, because in his time there was no one with an equally good alternative political conception to offer.

However, things changed under his immediate successors. Honorius III (1216–27), Gregory IX (1227–41) and Innocent IV (1243–54) found the Hohenstaufen Frederick II a fundamental opponent of Innocent's conception of the function of the papacy in Western Christendom.

(b) The challenge of the Hohenstaufens

The church politics of the thirteenth century were governed by this opposition. The eventual victory of the papacy of the high Middle Ages over the Hohenstaufens also sealed its own downfall. For despite its antique and conservative trappings, the system which the popes were fighting in Frederick II was one which was to redefine the relationship between *regnum* and *sacerdotium* at a territorial level. The future was to belong to it.

The Swabian Hohenstaufens, related to the Salians, were first of all passed over in the election of the king after the death of Henry V in 1125. The princes, interested in a balance between *sacerdotium* and *regnum* on the basis of the Concordat of Worms, elected the Saxon Count Lothair king (1125–37). Innocent II crowned him emperor in 1133. On the whole Lothair III pursued a policy which favoured the 'freedom of the church'. His successor, the first Hohenstafen, Conrad III (1138–52), introduced a cautious reorientation which was then fully implemented by his nephew, Frederick I Barbarossa (1152–90).

The new policy aimed at strengthening royal power in the empire and in Italy. The development of the church of the realm, which was taking on an increasingly feudal character, was halted; the Concordat of Worms was interpreted in favour of royal influence, and in a skilful personal policy bishops loyal to empire and king were appointed at elections. Rainald of Dassel (died 1167), the Chancellor and Archbishop of Cologne, can be seen as representative of the Hohenstaufen episcopate, which was in schism with the imperial popes. Frederick Barbarossa was in principle ready to recognize the honour of St Peter, i.e. the sovereignty of the church state and the dignity of the priesthood, as long as the priesthood accepted the imperial dignity. He went by the Ottonian and Salian model of order, which was deliberately combined with models from early Christianity, and the *sacrum imperium* was also used for propaganda purposes as an official title. This conception of Frederick's, who was crowned emperor in 1155, finally came to grief on the opposition of the cities of northern Italy, which were seeking to gain autonomy, and with whom Pope Alexander III was allied. Frederick himself died in Asia Minor on the Third Crusade in 1190.

His nephew, Frederick II, again took up the Italian policy and aimed to restore the old Christian *sacrum imperium*. Born in 1194, he was proclaimed king of Sicily in 1198, elected German king in 1212 and crowned emperor in 1220 by Pope Honorius III. He had acquired Sicily through his father, Henry VI, who had been crowned king of the southern Italian Norman kingdom as a result of his marriage with Constance of Sicily in 1194. Henry's early death (1197) put a rapid end to this far-reaching imperial policy. Constance (died 1198) recognized the pope as feudal lord and appointed Innocent III guardian of Frederick II.

There was a double election in the empire in 1198, in which Innocent intervened after some delay, taking sides with Otto of Brunswick against the Hohenstaufen Philip of Swabia. Otto IV prevailed only after the sudden death of Philip; he was crowned emperor by Innocent in Rome on 4 October 1209. The coronation liturgy produced for the occasion was a full expression of the papal view of the office of emperor as being at the service of the pope and the church.

Before his coronation, Otto had accepted all the pope's demands relating to the 'freedom of the church' in both the empire and the church state. However, no sooner was he secure in his power than he continued the Hohenstaufen policy and prepared an attack on southern Italy. Innocent excommunicated his former favourite in 1210 and now supported Frederick II, who was elected German king in 1212. Frederick gave the same promises as Otto IV and also solemnly recognized the pope's feudal rights over the kingdom of Sicily, which he was willing to renounce in favour of his son Henry. However, only in the empire did Frederick keep the promises he had given and in 1220 extended the freedoms of bishops in a statute 'in favour of the princes of the church', in order to secure their support. In Italy he pursued a policy of union which finally brought the whole peninsula under Hohenstaufen rule.

This set the programme for a conflict with the cities of northern Italy and above all with the Curia. This conflict quickly went beyond a dispute over matters of detail and was carried on by both sides with growing intensity. The concern of the papal side was the 'freedom of the church', which was felt to be threatened in three respects by Frederick. First, there was the incorporation of ecclesiastical institutions and individuals into the centralist government in the kingdom of Sicily. This was no more than the restoration of a royal church of the eleventh cenutry, but it was a kind of state church and moreover one in a kingdom under papal sovereignty. The second threat was to the sovereignty and autonomy of the church state, i.e. the political and material basis of an independent papal policy in Christendom. Thirdly, connected with this, was the challenge in principle to the role and position of the papacy. Deeply convinced of the superiority of his royal and imperial majesty, Frederick felt himself called by God to such a task. He attached the *sacerdotium* to spiritual activity or saw it as the extended arm of his rule. His model was the old conception of the unity of religion and politics, embodied in the person of the emperor. At least, that is how papal propaganda saw it, and Frederick II confirmed Christendom in this view by his passionate manifestos.

Gregory IX wanted to bring the fundamental dispute, which was interrupted by periods of compromise and temporary reconciliation, before the forum of Christendom and for this purpose summoned a council in Rome. However, Frederick prevented it by force. Having managed to flee from Rome, Innocent IV was able to convene the council in Lyons. On 17 July 1245 he had a bull of deposition proclaimed as a council decree; this not only released subjects from their oath of loyalty to the excommunicated emperor but also deprived Frederick of his royal and imperial office. Thus for the first time in history a pope directly applied sentence 12 of the *Dictatus papae*.

However, this battle had exhausted the spiritual powers of the papacy. The wider political perspective had been lost and turned into one of petty hatred against the Hohenstaufens, for whose annihilation the papacy sought allies. With the help of Charles of Anjou, a brother of the French king, the Hohenstaufens, who were fighting for their heritage in Italy, were defeated. Conradin, the last male heir, was executed in Naples on 29 October 1268.

The new king of Sicily and protector of the Roman church, Charles of Anjou (1265–85), had no intention of allowing the ideas of order held by the papacy of the high Middle Ages to influence his policy. And in the subsequent tensions, the papacy was completely trapped in the maelstrom of political clashes between powers with interests in the Italian conflict. For the time being the Curia had become completely incapable of action.

(c) The system in crisis

This lack of capacity to act is evident from the papal elections, which were sometimes preceded by long vacancies in the see. Here are some dates to illustrate the situation:

> Gregory IX, died 22 August 1241; Celestine IV, 25 October 1241 – 10 November 1241; Innocent IV, elected 25 June 1243; Clement IV, died 29 November 1268; Gregory X, elected 1 September 1271 (the longest vacancy in the see); Innocent V, 21 January 1276 – 26 June 1276; Hadrian V, 11 July 1276 – 18 August 1276; John XXI, 8 September 1276 – 20 May 1277; Nicholas IV, died 4 April 1292; Celestine V, elected 5 July 1294.

Superficially this could be explained by the lack of any regulations for elections. But the real reasons must be sought in the excessive political demands made on the college of cardinals. The battle against the Hohenstaufens had led in Italy to a splintering of political forces and the division into the Ghibellines and the Guelphs. The former sought to renew the greatness of Italy by attaching themselves to a strong (German) emperor; the latter saw the (Italian) papacy as the guarantee of peace in a land which had been parcelled up into small states. The formation of parties was reflected in the college of cardinals, and a further factor was the party of 'French' cardinals who had entered the college since Pope Urban IV (1261–64), who came from France; they sought their salvation in following France or Anjou southern Italy.

The precedence of the *sacerdotium* over the *regnum*, which was solemnly maintained in principle, had thus been overtaken by political reality even in the college of cardinals, and room for manoeuvre was limited to the question which of the different rival *regna* one was to follow. This important political question was further complicated by personal rivalries and the interests of the cardinals, who made themselves the champions of powerful and influential families like the Colonnas and the Orsinis. The honour of St Peter, which was still appealed to in the official declarations, had become an empty phrase. For the individual cliques were interested in family dynasties at the expense of the church state.

The varied and opposing interests, which could no longer be brought under any common heading, all clashed in a concentrated way in the papal elections. No regulations for election, however good, could have coped with them, as the introduction of the conclave showed.

The conclave was intended as a coercive measure with the aim of arriving at rapid agreement by putting pressure on the electors (seclusion, i.e. cramped and intolerable living conditions; rationing of food and drink). It was probably modelled on the various ordinances for conclaves in Italian communes. Previously the election of the pope had been an 'unregulated' process in which those involved came to agree on a candidate. The decree of the Third Lateran Council on papal elections (1179) had prescribed a two-thirds majority for nomination. The intention of this well-meant regulation was to prevent a double election, of the kind that had happened in 1159. But the regulation also made it difficult to reach agreement, especially when there was no agreed view on the solution to pending serious problems, or when the electoral college was internally split.

In the second half of the thirteenth century both these factors coincided. As there were no precise rules about the time, place, duration and procedure of papal elections, negotiations were dragged out and the matter was entrusted to negotiators. The individual parties attempted to get 'votes' by a great variety of means and tested the chances of individual candidates. They gave themselves time, and hoped for unforeseen events which could create a new situation and bring their own candidate or at least an acceptable compromise candidate to the fore.

The political and social stability of Italy and the church state were affected by being drawn into this 'game'. The communes, which were exasperated by it, intervened, and forced a conclave on the cardinals. The best known case of this kind was the conclave at Viterbo in August 1271, which led to the election of Gregory X (1271–76). Gregory had the compulsory measure legalized by the Second Council of Lyons (1274), which proclaimed it a new papal electoral ordinance. Hadrian V, who was elected on 11 July 1276 and died as early as 18 August, abolished the conclave ordinance as putting unbearable pressure on the cardinals and infringing their freedom of choice. It became valid law again only under Boniface VIII.

The conclave could not be an effective instrument for overcoming the crisis in which the papacy of the high Middle Ages found itself. With or without the conclave, the previous practice was followed when no agreement could be reached: the problem was postponed by electing a very old cardinal or one without any influence or stature. In the first instance a short pontificate could be expected; in the second there was a possibility that previous policies would be continued and existing power and influence be maintained. Again the older and politically weaker personalities were suitable for this, especially the 'pious' cardinals from the orders, who had no political support in the church state and in other Italian states.

The most spectacular papal election of the papacy of the high Middle Ages as it went into decline, that of Celestine V on 5 July 1294, belongs in this connection. Peter of Morrone, a hermit from the Abruzzi, with no political experience whatsoever, was thought of merely as a man of straw in the hands of rival groups which were blocking each other. One celebrated Celestine as *papa angelicus* in its propaganda and in this way assured itself of the support of the Franciscan spirituals, who were naive enough to see Celestine's election as the end of a politicized and secularized church and the dawn of the 'church of the Spirit'. In reality the hermit, who took up residence in Naples, was a helpless tool in the hand of King Charles II, who misused him ruthlessly in the interest of the Anjous.

Under the leadership of Cardinal Benedict Gaetani, a front of cardinals now rapidly formed. It was also Benedict who suggested to the pope that he should resign, and produced legal grounds for his doing so. On 13 December 1294 Celestine handed in his resignation. Under the impact of their experience with Celestine and the Anjous, the cardinals in conclave quickly agreed on Benedict Gaetani, a prominent personality well fitted for leadership. Boniface VIII (1292–1303) was a statesman of stature, with diplomatic experience and considerable legal training. With a strong hand he restored order to the church state, consolidated its battered finances, and attempted to intervene in order to bring balance and mediation in the crisis-torn area of southern Italy and in the war between England and France. However, in all questions relating to the freedom of the church he was a prisoner of the principles of the Petrine apostolic principle, which canon law had extended into the political sphere.

In rigidly maintaining these principles against King Philip IV of France (1285–1314), Boniface, and with him the papacy of the high Middle Ages, came to grief. Granted the French monarchy was not making any imperialistic claims, but it insisted on the sovereignty of its national state. So Philip refused to recognize the prohibition of his taxation of clergy which was issued in the bull *Clericis laicos* (25 February 1296). In the name of the autonomy of royal power he protested against the bulls *Ausculta fili* of 5 December 1301 and *Unam Sanctam* of 18 November 1302, which argued that the subjection of the *regnum* to the *sacerdotium* was necessary for salvation, and appealed to a general council. Anticipating his solemn excommunication on 8 September 1303, on 7 September Philip captured Boniface at Anagni with a view to having him condemned as a false pope at a council. Philip found zealous support for the imprisonment of the pope and the plan for his deposition among the cardinals of the house of Colonna and also the French spirituals. The latter were hostile to Boniface, whom they blamed for the resignation of Celestine; the former were indignant at this Gaetani pope from the petty nobility who had dared to snatch the power of their family for the church state. The coalition of such different papal opponents blackened the memory of the failed pope with extravagant propaganda.

4. The hierarchical claim of the papacy to jurisdiction

The Gregorian reform had been backed by an ecclesiology orientated on salvation history which understood the church as the body of Christ ruled by the priesthood and associated responsibility for the world with spiritual office. As a result, a new definition of the relationship between papal authority and royal power had become necessary. In the course of the twelfth and thirteenth centuries the papacy's claim to priestly rule was developed from the principles of the Petrine apostolic principle and with a view to particular functions in church politics. It was Innocent III in particular who defined the competences and sought to give them validity under the favourable conditions of the hour.

(a) The secular competence of the pope

The papal authority was not limited by any secular power in the priestly-ecclesiastical sphere. Now the pope, rather than the emperor, was seen as the head of the priestly hierarchy and the principle of the ecumenical unity of Christendom. All spheres of church administration and legislation, the defence and the dissemination of faith, fell under papal authority. Papal decretals defined doctrine and set the norms for discipline.

Relations with Byzantium were of course also deeply affected by the Petrine apostolic principle and *de facto* deteriorated to the point of a formal schism. The excommunication of the patriarch by the papal legates on 16 July 1054 was initially just one of the frequent gestures in the provisional breaking off of diplomatic relations.

However, papal competence in the secular sphere, which was derived from the idea of the pope as vicɔr of Christ, was equally important for Western Christendom.

The issue involved differing competences in four different spheres: 1. in the church state; 2. in the papal feudal states; 3. in the bestowing of the imperial crown; 4. in intervening in any exercise of secular rule.

The pope's secular competence remained unlimited first in the church state, in which he was sovereign ruler. The church state had explicitly been excluded from the agreements at Sutri in 1111. The patrimony of Peter was thus not regarded as a regale of the king. The political sovereignty of the church state was no longer under discussion and was also sealed under imperial law with the Concordat of Worms in 1122. Reference was still made to the Donation of Constantine as historical legitimation for the papal states, but the donation was interpreted as a restitution. The reinterpretation took place in the course of the twelfth century. According to it, Constantine merely restored to the Roman church what Christ had assigned to it by virtue of the Petrine office. The restitution theory presupposed reflection on the precedence of the *sacerdotium* over the *regnum* and a further development of the Gregorian reform's concept of the church by twelfth-century canon law. For if the church state were to have derived from a donation it would have had to be conceded, first, that the *imperium* had to be regarded as older than the *sacerdotium* and thus as a higher institution, and, secondly, that the donor could take the donation back again. At all events, the secular rule of the church would have had its roots in a concession by the *imperium*.

Secondly, the papacy had secular competence in relation to the papal feudal states. These were the kingdoms whose rulers for very different reasons had handed them over to St Peter, to receive them back again from the pope as fiefs. The best-known papal feudal state after 1059 was the Norman kingdom in Southern Italy. Bulgaria, Bohemia, Castile and England had also at times been in such a state feudal dependency. It need hardly be stressed that the papal supremacy inferred from this mostly existed only in theory, and could hardly be implemented in practice.

Thirdly, there was a special competence which extended into the secular sphere in the bestowal of the imperial crown, in other words the calling of a ruler to imperial office. This right, inferred from the view that the pope was Christ's representative, underlay the translation theory as interpreted by the pope and the church (to be distinguished from the renewal of empire, the theory according according to which the *imperium* had passed from the Romans to the Franks and through the Saxons to the Germanic kingdom, see above 36). According to this theory, the Christian *imperium* was not simply the continuation of the ancient pagan empire. It came to be truly defined by being Christianized, and in this way attained a new and higher quality. However, this quality was mediated by papal authority, which therefore had a higher dignity than imperial power as the effective cause and goal of the empire. The nature and functions of imperial rule were thus defined by the quality of the Christian *imperium*. The emperor called by the pope was entrusted with the defence and protection of the church as its supreme advocate. Thus the position of emperor was interpreted as an office in the church.

Fourthly, the pope had the general competence to give instructions to any secular power. This competence was grounded in a threefold subordination of the temporal to the spiritual. This was: (a) With respect to the goal of all rule, which was at the service of the defence of the church and the maintenance of justice. (b) With respect to its subjects: through the activity of the *sacerdotium* these were Christians and subject to the priesthood in all spheres relating to their eternal salvation. (c) With respect to sin, because of which rulers had to be controlled and corrected, since sin easily led rulers to misuse their power, to injustice and tyranny. The *sacerdotium* had to take steps against this corruption by sin in order to serve the cause of justice and peace.

These four realms need to be taken into account in any answer to the question of the nature of the mediaeval papal *imperium*. This rule cannot simply be called 'rule of the world' in the sense of a theocratic monism, as the Anonymous of York required for the king. Strictly speaking, it is not a papal hierocracy either, but an order of precedence in the framework of the hierarchical ordering of the world and salvation. Here creation was ordered by salvation. However, as redemption did not simply do away with creation, priestly power, which was derived from the rule of Christ, did not displace secular power, which, on the basis of biblical passages like Romans 13.1, was part of the order of creation. Therefore the fact that the pope was the vicar of Christ did not give him a comprehensive theocracy.

The *sacerdotium* had no competence to give instructions in purely secular matters (like feudal law). However, in so far as the creation was interpreted in terms of redemption there could be no autonomous secular power. Rather, its function was to be of service to the redemption 'administered' by the priesthood. However, this function of service, aimed at the same goal, did not deprive the secular authority of any relative independence.

(b) The theory of the two swords

In the course of the early and high Middle Ages there were various images for the relationship between spiritual and secular power: body – soul; sun – moon; spiritual sword – secular sword. The religious-political exegesis of the Middle Ages could refer to Luke 22.38 for the famous simile of the sword. Boniface VIII's bull *Unam sanctam* can be regarded as a classic summary of the papal political theory of the two powers. This states: 'So both swords are in the power of the church, the spiritual and the physical. The latter is to be wielded for the church, the former by the church. The latter belongs to the priest, the former is in the hand of kings and warriors, but at the bidding of the priest and by his permission.' From the wording alone, one could infer a theocratic monism according to which all secular power is mediated by the priesthood. But given the historical development of the theory, which can be clearly seen in the decretists of the twelfth century and with Innocent III, the simile of the two swords is also clearly about the hierarchical order which takes account of the relative independence of the secular sword.

By virtue of its origin and purpose, the 'reality' of the spiritual sword of the church does not lie in the temporal sphere. The image of the spiritual sword is focussed on the priestly *potestas circa corpus*

Christi reale (see p.16), i.e. on the sanctification of the individual Christian and of Christendom which is to be achieved through the sacraments. However, this sanctification does not remain an internal matter. It is externalized in the visible realm and makes men and women the legally constituted corporation of the visible church. So the attitude of faith has a legal effect. Here the church's power of the keys extends to the visible sphere and becomes the power of law, compulsion and punishment.

So the spiritual sword works at two levels. The first level is purely inward, spiritual and supernatural. The second has an external sphere which can be legally defined. It can even be called the church's material sword. All penitential conditions imposed on sinners come under the penal authority of this sword. However, in the political theory of the division of authority the church's power of the keys relates only to transgressions which relate to public order, peace and the faith, i.e. the activities of rebels, agitators, peacebreakers, men of violence and heretics. The priesthood established the fact of the crime and imposed excommunication on the perpetrators, which was meant to move them to repentance and penitence. But the pronouncing of spiritual punishment had no effect on impenitent perpetrators of violence and disturbers of the peace. For while the saying about the material sword imposed a punishment which extended into the public realm, it was not intrinsically capable of putting an end to the criminal act. So church punishment remained in the sphere of words and morality. It only stated a punishment for the common good, which was defined in terms of Christian faith. To impose the punishment it was dependent upon the temporal sword of secular power. This then had to put the power bestowed on it by God at the disposal of the church.

In the interlocking of secular and spiritual authority we have two authorities which are different in character and only combine in the exercise of power. The secular authority did not put its means of power, the temporal sword (the image for secular power in the service of the order of creation), at the disposal of punitive expeditions defined and limited by the church. Here it was acting on behalf of the church and was helping the church's material sword to be effective.

In the light of the way in which the two authorities supplemented each other in their functions, we can say that the secular power received the material sword from the hand of the church. So similarly two functional spheres were to be distinguished in the use of the temporal sword. First there was the competence of the secular power which not been mediated by the church, and then there was the sphere in which it acted on behalf of the church. In the latter case the temporal sword became the material sword mediated and legitimated by the church. Only in this sense did the secular authority receive the secular sword from the hands of the priesthood.

Scholars argue over whether Boniface VIII and Innocent IV before him had this relationship in mind. They are often thought to have held a papal theocratic monism which quite a few decretalists advanced at the end of the thirteenth century. With them the boundaries were blurred and the material sword of the church was identified with the temporal sword. The material sword which kings were to wield on behalf of the priesthood became the temporal sword which was mediated only through the church. The church's comprehensive authority to instruct and the threefold subordination of all rule to the priesthood became an ecclesiastical-papal monism. During the twelfth century and the beginning of the thirteenth century things had not yet got that far.

We can also see an unprecedented secularization in the functional connection of the secular sword with the spiritual sword, a transformation of the spiritual church into a powerful secularized church. However, these are evaluations of a different age or of an ascetic view of the church which was not that of the majority at the time. Until well into the thirteenth century, the spiritual elite accepted and defended the comprehensive papal competence to intervene as a valid expression of the divine plan of salvation. So we cannot speak over-hastily of the spiritual being seduced by power, but have to evaluate the hierarchical claim to leadership here as an idealistic utopian attempt to bind the power in the world to the spiritual and establish righteousness and peace in Christendom.

However, the papacy regularly came up against enemies on its way to this goal. They had to be fought, and they became violent and self-confident in the course of the battle. The Spirit was appealed to only as a source of power or, as in the case of Boniface VIII, when appeals were made to the principles of a system of order which in the new and changed political conditions had forfeited both meaning and function.

IV

The Defence and Deepening of the Faith in the Church of the High Middle Ages

The papacy saw its role as one of defending and extending the faith, deepening it and renewing it in Western Christendom. It was as natural for the popes here to identify their own concerns with the faith as it was that their tasks should be seen in political terms. This attitude found typical expression in the Crusades and the fight against heresy. Papal initiatives played a leading role in these enterprises. The attitude can be seen less clearly in relation to the renewal and deepening of faith. Here scholarship and piety developed a dynamic of their own under the pressure of the social and cultural upheavals of the time. In this process papal and synodical instructions served less to initiate than to stimulate, regulate or discipline.

In the long run it proved impossible for papal leadership to mobilize and discipline all the social strata of Christendom. The forces which were unleashed by religious appeals eventually became independent, contrary to the original intentions. That is true not only of the crusades but also of reforms within the church. They embraced particular social groups and became combined with cultural and political interests. The pressure towards reform from the one succeeded at the cost of the other and thus led to new conflicts and tasks. We need to note this interaction carefully in connection with the defence and deepening of the faith which aimed at the pastoral mobilization of the forces for renewing faith and life.

1. Pastoral renewal: agents – institutions – groups

The First Lateran Council (1123) can be called an epilogue to the Gregorian Reform. Once again all the demands relating to pastoral care were enumerated in the canons of the council. With the shift in the reform from monasticism to the episcopate, it was the episcopal and clerical institutions which were primarily charged with its implementation. A series of important steps were taken in conjunction with it. Church law described the episcopal and clerical institutions as corporations, thus taking account of the notion of the freedom of the church and the ecclesiastical nature of the spiritual office.

Since it was the most important corporate institution at diocesan level, the cathedral chapter shared in the government of the diocese as an extension of the role of the bishop. In the twelfth century, the cathedral schools and the monastic schools were the main vehicles of the spiritual and academic life of the time.

The bond between the bishop and the clergy who acted on his behalf restored the principle of episcopal oversight of the clergy. This resulted in a further division of the diocese into archdeaconries and deaneries, and the delegation of episcopal tasks relating to administration and jurisdiction. However, the institutions involved differed widely from district to district. In establishing or developing them the tendency was to begin from existing institutions. The spiritual and pastoral rights and duties of the parishes were prescribed. The definition of the pastor as the priest of the parish meant that his sole duty, for which alone he was authorized, was to perform spiritual actions. Compulsory measures and excommunications of parish priests became a norm in church law.

However, the 'freedom of the church' sought by the Gregorian reform did not come about lower down the church (in parishes and daughter churches). In theory, lay rule of the church had come to an end, but the old practice lived on vigorously under new names. The church law of the time distinguished between *donum altaris* (gift of the altar) and *donum fundi* (gift of property) in respect of these church posts. The *donum altaris* stressed the spiritual character of priestly office and made institution to pastoral service by the bishop compulsory. The *donum fundi* took account of the rights of the previous lord of the proprietary church (or the one who was to found the church). Founders of church property were left a series of rights ranging from presentation and nomination of the incumbent to material enjoyment of the benefice (rights of patronage). So the patron retained some influence on his church through the church property associated with the office. Moreover the stipend attached to the *donum fundi* also lost any direct relationship to pastoral duties. It could be separated from these and assigned for the use of a third party. The beneficiary from the benefice income then had only the obligation to appoint a vicar and remunerate him for fulfilling the spiritual and pastoral tasks incumbent upon the benefice. In the course of the twelfth century the exploitation of parish church property by other institutions and persons constantly increased. By the late Middle Ages it had become the rule. In the twelfth century, the monasteries and canonical foundations were those which were most frequently favoured with it.

Of course this material exploitation of the lower reaches of the church had a paralysing effect on the pastoral care of the lower classes. Still, their religious needs, too, were not particularly developed. Their cultic observance was rooted in customs connected with crises. Pastoral care remained tailored to that. An educated clergy of a high spiritual level was not in keeping with this social milieu.

However, such a clergy had become necessary for the new social classes which had been slowly forming since the middle of the eleventh century from the mass of subjects who living in a great variety of relationships with different degrees of dependence. Those concerned were first of all the nobility in service and then – some time later – the urban middle classes.

(a) The reform orders and the nobility

The striking encouragement of canonical and monastic institutions by popes and bishops at the expense of the lower levels of the church was connected with the nobility in service, who established themselves as a new class of nobility below the old aristocracy. In the course of the twelfth century the shift of the reform to the episcopate issued in a new link between the monasteries and the nobility and produced the last great blossoming of mediaeval monasticism, which was a very important factor in the religious-ecclesiastical and cultural-spiritual life of the time.

In piety and life-style the new and lesser nobility followed the pattern of the older and high nobility. For a long time the monastery had played a major role in the world of the old nobility. The new nobles also wanted to have monasteries for similar purposes. This is where the reform orders came in.

At first sight the alliance of reform orders and the nobility seems to be a contradiction. For as a result of its beginnings, reform monasticism had an ascetic, eremitical orientation, and in contrast to earlier monasticism rejected social and ecclesiastical functions. The monasteries wanted neither oratories nor churches (= pastoral care and income). Their aim was not to turn towards the world but to turn from the world; they sought religious and economic self-sufficiency. But it was precisely this monastic poverty and modesty which in the long run made the new monasticism apt for a bond with the nobility. For now it had become less expensive to found monasteries. Both old and new nobility seized the chances offered here to excel in piety by founding monasteries, and thus gaining domestic or family monasteries. In addition there was the enthusiasm for the Crusades and the distress which followed. Crusaders vowed to found monasteries, and once again their pious concern was not unrelated to preoccupations with power: by transferring their property they guaranteed control of it and provided for the support of their families. In many places several noblemen formed a kind of consortium, in particular for founding convents (in which their daughters could live).

The closer the ties between the monastery and the nobility became, the closer the monasteries came once again to having possessions; here the transfer of the use of proprietary churches belonging to the lay nobility or of churches of which the nobility were patrons provided most of the material resources. So in the course of the twelfth century a wide-ranging social network developed which brought a wide stratum of the nobility into contact with monastic culture. The nobles were influenced by its piety, and in the course of this reciprocal encounter the original asceticism of the founding generation of monks lost its sharpness and gradually became more cultivated.

These monasteries were also much more closely connected with the papacy of the time and its concerns. The popes called on the canons and the Cistercians above all to perform specific commissions and engage in large-scale actions, like preaching Crusades and fighting against heretics. By contrast, direct pastoral care was less important, even among the canons, except in the cities which were coming into being, where numerous smaller communities of canons were founded in the course of the twelfth century.

However, while monastic life was blossoming and monastic culture and piety were influencing the nobility, there was a pastoral emergency in the cities, where the religious situation was reaching crisis point.

(b) The mendicant orders and the cities

With time lags and a west-east or north-south movement which needs to be taken into consideration, the urbanization which came about in Europe in the course of the twelfth and thirteenth centuries called into being a new social stratum which acquired great significance for the later Middle Ages. Alongside the proprietary landowners there appeared a new group which was different legally, politically and in economic terms: the autonomous urban citizens as a self-administering body bound by an oath. This new group awakened cultural and religious needs which could no longer be fulfilled by the existing church institutions and personnel and initially led to a religious and pastoral crisis.

The crisis had roots in the organization and social role of the institutions, aspects each of which influenced the other. The organizational crisis arose from the mismatch between the new settlements and the existing parish organization. The latter was complete and its responsibilities had been laid down. As a result, many of the small and medium-sized towns in Germany which came into being had no parish churches. The inhabitants were still part of the parish of a village parish church or had to look for a parish church in the fields outside the town. Both these types of church, and the parish church in the older cities, which had grown up around episcopal or monastic churches, were in the hands of ecclesiastical or monastic institutions. Institutionally they were part of the monastic or the episcopal church of the aristocracy. This church order and mentality provided no place for a civic church. From a social perspective, the churches as institutions had been taken over by the aristocracy.

The ascetic monastic movement appeared on the scene once again to cope with the ecclesiastical and religious crises in the towns and cities, performing similar functions to those which it had had to perform earlier for the leading classes of the time. For this to happen, there was a need for a link between the city and the monasteries. This urbanization of the monastic form of life took place in several stages. The mendicant orders were the result of this important process of transformation. At the end of the thirteenth century they had become a respected and influential institution of urban society, and with their imposing churches put a new stamp on the image of the city which could not to be overlooked.

There were various mendicant orders in the thirteenth century. The four classical and most important are: the Dominicans or Order of Preachers, founded by St Dominic of Caleruega (died 1221); the Franciscans or Minorites founded by St Francis of Assisi (died 1226); the Augustinian hermits, who came into being from a combination of various Italian eremitical associations which had been approved by Pope Alexander in 1256; and the Carmelites, who came into being as a result of the transplantation of the order from the Holy Land to Europe and its reorganization by Simon Stock (died 1265). The beginnings of the individual orders initially had little to do with their rapid transformation into successful urban mendicant orders (except in the case of the Dominicans). The grouping of the various orders under the term 'mendicant' came about as a result of church law. Despite various features peculiar to particular orders, the mendicant orders displayed the following characteristics: they renounced possessions and had the right to beg, granted by church law; and they were groups independent of any place in the sense that all the members were bound together regardless of the monastery to which they belonged in an association directed by a magister general (with a corporate constitution): here the training of clergy destined for pastoral care was built into the constitution.

The common roots were provided by the religious movement of the time, in the wake of which the ascetic and monastic tradition developed further the Gospel idea of the apostolic life from eremitical asceticism to apostolic asceticism, expressed in the life of the itinerant preacher, and gave it form in the demand for evangelical poverty. The various religious and social needs of the urban civic community or those propertied classes which set the tone were factors in their transformation into succesful urban orders responsible for pastoral care.

Like the lords who owned land, the cities as corporate bodies sought religious legitimation and sanctification. The mendicant orders were brought into service for the various functions which were called for in connection with this. The institutions of the older monastic communities were hardly suited to perform such functions. For as monasteries with property over which they exercised rule they would have formed an alien body in urban society. A community without property which lived by begging and had no fixed income could fit more easily into urban life. The forms of 'begging' rapidly brought in money to pay for the great city monasteries of the mendicants: their subsistence was guaranteed by gifts from the upper clases of the city. This was a kind of democratization of the pious foundations. Whereas previously only the landowning nobility had been able to found churches and monasteries, now those other classes (merchants, entrepreneurs, and so on) could take part in this meritorious work. The sum of these foundations, supplemented by the alms of ordinary people who had benefited from the growing urban economy, was enough to safeguard the existence of the new orders, whose cost-intensive organization of study and great monastic buildings swallowed up large amounts of money.

Thus after the 1250s, alongside the urban parish churches, the monasteries of the mendicant orders came into being as new centres to meet the religious and ecclesiastical needs of urban society. These needs were primarily cultic: the pious prayer and ascetic life-style of the monks contributed to the well-being and salvation of the urban community. Here the monasteries of the mendicant orders took on the function of the domestic and family monasteries of the nobility. Soon their churches and cloisters were the places in which the urban upper classes preferred to be buried. This religious and social function can be demonstrated from the beginning in addition to the pastoral function of the orders in giving religious instruction through preaching and confession.

Because of their apostolic and ascetic ideal, the rising mendicant orders sought to preach penitence. The original lay itinerant preaching was clericalized by Dominic and combined with an academic training. The other orders rapidly followed the Dominicans. This put the mendicant orders in a position to help the bishops to fulfil the prescriptions of the Fourth Lateran Council (1215) to appoint teachers and preachers. Until well beyond the middle of the thirteenth century, the bishops supported them in their work. From the beginning the mendicant orders had been encouraged by the papacy. A wealth of papal mandates and privileges smoothed their way towards a role in pastoral care which was regularly disputed by the clergy of the parish churches.

Here preaching was not an issue, since hitherto it had played only a subordinate role in pastoral care and was really the task of the bishops, who from old had been regarded as the preachers. The stumbling block was the sovereign rights of the parishes, especially the right to hold public worship, the right to bury and the authority to hear confessions. Economic interests apart, the previous monopoly of the parish priest was infringed here. The weakness of the parish church which went with the rise of the mendicant orders could only suit the cities. As a rule the countless small disputes involving the mendicant orders in the cities were over claims to establish communities which were backed by an alliance of the papacy and the city.

Pastoral activity was not only encouraged by the popes but also safeguarded by law, in that the mendicant orders received a canonical mission in the form of a papal charge. This interference in the competence of the bishop was possible only on the basis of the concept of Petrine apostolic ecclesiology, in which the pope was responsible for the interests of the whole church. The right to preach freely regardless of any diocesan boundaries which was claimed by the lay itinerant preachers of the end of the twelfth and beginning of the thirteenth centuries and contested by the bishops as heretical was taken up by the pope and introduced into church order as a papal commissioning of the mendicant orders at a supra-diocesan level.

For this reason, the theologians and canon lawyers of the mendicant orders in the thirteenth and early fourteenth centuries were also resolute defenders of the papal primacy of jurisdiction, and tended to see the pope as the source of all spiritual authority. Moreover, with the urbanization of monasticism as represented by the mendicants, the papacy also acquired an 'auxiliary troop' whose numbers often swayed the balance. International in constitution and training, mobile and educated, the mendicants had an advantage in gaining information which gave them an important role in the shaping of public opinion. More efficient than individual secular clergy, canons and Cistercians, they could be used for large-scale papal mission projects, like the 're-Catholicizing' of the Greeks, the preaching of Crusades and the fight against heretics.

2. Scholarship and piety

The changes which took place in the social and cultural spheres during the twelfth and thirteenth centuries also made an unmistakable mark on scholarship and piety. To begin with, the monastic-canonicial institutions had considerable significance in these two spheres, which were closely connected. Over time, academic life shifted into the cities and led to a religious culture which largely had an urban stamp.

(a) The blossoming of academic theology

The twelfth and thirteenth century were splendid times for theology. There was a progressive development leading to the formation of schools and the transformation of theology into an academic discipline. The institutions in which the theology of the schools was done were initially the monasteries and canonical foundations, and then the cathedral and monastic schools which were coming into being. Finally there was a new institution – the university. The institutional changes to the schools also affected the aims and content of theology.

All in all this was a kind of pre-scholasticism which in different forms developed into early scholasticism and from that into high scholasticism, achieving maturity in the second half of the thirteenth century. In the transition from early to high scholasticism a distinction needs to be made between a technical and an organizational side, which conditioned and permeated each other.

Authoritative texts were the basis for all the knowledge of the schools at the time. Every discipline created an appropriate textbook for itself. In theology the authoritative texts were made up of holy scripture and the tradition of the fathers. The interpretation of scripture with and through the norm of the fathers produced the theological style of early scholasticism.

Technically, theology was done by means of glossing (*glossare* = to explain a text: *glossa* = the explanation of a text). The individual forms of glossing (commentating) produced the various glosses. The great period of glossing began in the Carolingian era. This literature came to a peak in the twelfth century. The method was to use the three steps of *littera-sensus-sententia*: in other words, the results of the glossing of a text were introduced into the traditional material as a new gloss (= *sententia*). The twofold structure of the literal and spiritual senses, which had been developed in late antiquity and taken over from there, was used to grasp and deepen the meaning. The scheme of four senses, which distinguished between literal, allegorical (typological), moral and anagogical (eschatological) senses was very widespread. (There was a famous verse in the late Middle Ages: *Littera gesta docet, quid credas allegoria; moralis quid agas, quo tendas anagogia*: 'the literal sense teaches what happened, allegory what you may believe, the moral sense what you may do, the anagogical sense the direction in which you may go'.) By the twelfth century the various sets of senses had already been catalogued and put into lexicons. Here patristic exegesis was abundantly evident.

This was generally used to elucidate the meaning in the gloss. Of course the whole tradition of patristic theology was no longer available. In the cultural decline from late antiquity to the early Middle Ages this writing was deflowered, and the excerpts were included in anthologies and collections of sentences from the fathers. Augustine, Ambrose and Gregory the Great were the most quoted authors. In the twelfth century the collections from the fathers became much richer, which suggests a considerable learned readership.

Anselm of Laon (died 1117), a great teacher with many pupils, brought the hey-day of glossatory literature, which in the exegesis of the schools reflected on and assimilated the material of a tradition that had become very much broader. The achievements of his school were the result of a high level of literary education. That is also true of the other schools of the twelfth century. These achievements would not have been possible without a perfect grasp of the seven liberal arts. Grammar and rhetoric above all played a prominent role in this 'philology of the Holy Spirit'.

Despite the guild of the schools, there was still room for personal style, for aesthetics in form and content. 'Monastic theology' has become established as a collective term for this scholastic-type theology practised in the cathedral and monastic schools. It included not only glossatory literature but also the numerous treatises on relevant and contemporary themes into which the results of glossing were introduced, as they were into the broad literature of monastic edification. This 'monastic theology' is a reflection and expression of the height of monasticism in the twelfth century. The cultivation of scholarship was put at the service of the love of God. The letter was to be illuminated by the spirit (*spiritus*) in its manifold wealth of meaning. This exegesis, based on a symbolic and Platonic understanding of being, provided the building blocks for a spiritual cosmos of which monastic culture felt itself to be a part.

However, the scholastic element in monastic theology extended beyond the cosmos of scholarly training and took a further step by transforming theology into a science. Abelard (died 1142) marks the important break. He rejected philological learning as useless and called for the construction of an academic theology through speculation. No intellectual problems caused by the tension between the understanding in search of faith or faith in search of understanding could be resolved by the endless accumulation of quotations from authorities. Intellectual effort was needed. The philology of the liberal arts became philosophy. Logic and dialectic became all-important as the prime means of rational technique. They helped towards an adequate understanding of a structure of words and meaning and the resolution of existing contradictions.

The resolution of contradictions had in any case become an urgent task for the schools. Canon law was also working on this. The very title of Gratian's *Concordantia discordantium canonum* indicates the issue: the disparate and contradictory material of the tradition had to be harmonized and interpreted in the light of present needs. The collections of sentences from the fathers also had to be harmonized and systematized. The beginnings of a dogmatic textbook were created with the new collections arranged by themes. In 1152 Peter Lombard created a very well chosen thematic collection of this kind. In the course of the thirteenth century his *Quattuor libri sententiarum* became an official book for teaching and use in the schools and remained so for three centuries. The more conservative glossing theology orientated on erudition distanced itself from this development. It criticized the systematization of scriptural theology and the rationalism of the methods, which endangered the edifying character of theology by disturbing the traditional structure and statements and putting them in question.

However, in the new intellectual movement of the time the future belonged to rational methods, even more so after the West had been made familiar with the works of Aristotle. The seven liberal arts were transformed into scholastic philosophy in the course of interpretation of Aristotle. Albertus Magnus (died 1280) did a great service for theology here; Thomas Aquinas (died 1274) completed the interpretation of Aristotle in theology. With him high scholasticism reached its heyday and the new literary genres of the school achieved maturity.

These were governed by the role of the theological teacher in *lectio*, *disputatio* and *praedicatio*. Even in high scholasticism, the *magister* had to expound the text. He simply continued to glossing it with new means and aims. The end-product of this work on the text was not longer a new gloss but the sentence. The texts read were Holy Scripture and the *Sentences* of Peter Lombard. Thus commentaries on scripture and on the *Sentences* were the most important literary genres and the most extensive works of high scholastic theology. However, in these commentaries the text merely served as a formal framework on which a meaning was constructed. This was especially true of the great commentaries on the *Sentences*, in which the authority of the fathers was subordinated to the authority of reason.

In the disputations, the teacher took up problems of the day and intellectual questions independently of the texts and clarified them in the magistral *disputatio de quolibet*. The truth confirmed by *lectio* and *disputatio* was introduced into the scholastic school preaching.

On the academic, organizational side of the development we must again begin with the monasteries. The schools sought to teach by the three stages of *lectio*, *meditatio* and *oratio*. Their concern for a deeper understanding of scripture necessitated technical methods and specialization of knowledge, and this led to their becoming independent. The great theological literature of the twelfth century came into being in these schools, which were only loosely associated with the cathedral and monastic institutions. The fact that masses of students flocked to the famous teachers at the cathedral, foundations and monastic schools of France and northern Italy led to a further degree of independence. Around the end of the twelfth century, teachers and pupils became completely emancipated from previous institutional frameworks and formed the *universitas studentium et magistrorum*, in order to regulate their own interests as a corporation.

The issue here was their special legal status, their privileges and rights over against bishops, provosts, abbots and rulers of cities. Papal, imperial and royal privileges guaranteed the exempt status that they had achieved. To this legal significance of the 'university' as a freed corporation with self-administration was added the special character of the school. A *studium particulare* at a particular place for which the bishop was responsible became a *studium generale* of Western Christendom in which the pope took the place of the bishop. This comprised 'general studies', and at the end of the course prescribed by statutes, those who qualified as 'doctor of theology' received a licence to teach 'anywhere in the world'.

The activity of the teacher was institutionalized in the chair, the magistral *cathedra*. The number of these chairs varied from university to university. But there were several *magistri* in the large schools, each of whom had to deal with the same material. So there was as yet no specialization by theological disciplines. The organizational rivalry of the *magistri* led to rivalry over the content of courses.

Despite all the uniformity in formal and technical matters, this left a good deal of scope for a plurality of views and standpoints which found expression in academic discussion and polemic. Through the mendicant orders, which soon came to have chairs in Paris and elsewhere, the formation of particular theological schools was deepened and institutionalized, following theological trends. For the chairs at the universities were regarded as the culmination of the organization of the study of the order as a whole, which by stages and in various branches reached down into individual houses of the order.

In this organizational structure the theological system of a famous teacher like that of St Thomas among the Dominicans or St Bonaventure among the Franciscans could be prescribed as the norm for studies in provinces and houses. However, we should not exaggerate the coherence of this situation. There was no uniform Dominican or even Franciscan theology.

Generally speaking, the mendicant orders must be seen as having played an important role in disseminating scholastic literature and adapting it for pastoral work. For the transformation of theology into a science at the high schools had largely detached it from direct practical and pastoral needs. The theological reflection which took place at a high level with its results expressed in the language of the schools had to be rewritten. Moreover, more usable textbooks were needed for the instruction given at a lower level. Comprehensive *Summae* and *Compendia* were written to meet these. One widespread example was the *Compendium theologicae veritatis* of the Strasbourg Dominican Hugo Ripelin, who died in 1268. Thomas Aquinas' *Summa Theologiae* was also written as a compendium to be used outside the schools. However, Thomas wanted his students to join in finding the results. Most of the simplified summaries of and excerpts from the theological literature which were widespread at the time were only interested in the results of academic learning and research. The same is true of the many handbooks on moral theology which were written as *Summae de casibus* or *Summae de poenitentia* and which went into circulation in abbreviated editions.

From the second half of the thirteenth century this broad theological literature orientated on praxis was at the same time the new edifying literature form on which the piety of those classes in the pastoral care of the mendicant orders drew.

(b) Piety

At first glance the piety was enormously varied and produced an uninterrupted series of texts and exercises. But we must not overlook. the formal unity in the multiplicity. This profited from the common religious and spiritual culture: Latin as the language in liturgy and in the schools. As monasticism was also the vehicle of education, academic concerns also had an effect on religious literature (scholarship and the longing for God). Only with rational and speculative scholasticism did a slow differentiation begin between learning and piety, though this was again neutralized by the monastic life-style and edifying literature, which even in the scholastic transcription kept to the old models.

So there was no radical break in piety despite the different far-reaching social and cultural changes. The reinterpretation of scripture and tradition which had become necessary on each occasion took place in the traditional monastic structure, supported by a society which as a whole remained rooted in the traditional religious notions sanctioned by the church. The exceptions to this were the various heretical movements of the twelfth century and the beginning of the thirteenth century which sometimes embraced broader circles. Their reintegration into the general consensus over piety was achieved not least through the mendicant orders, who as disseminators of the old monastic piety among the urban population showed them new forms and content for religious devotion.

The various religous prayer texts and topics derived from monastic needs and in basic form already point back to the early Middle Ages. The monastic ideal of persisting in constant prayer was not only expanded in seven separate times of common prayer but was also supplemented by both communal and private exercises. The norm was the daily office, in which the Psalms were the most important material of prayer. As 'sacred words' they were used for additional offices and private prayers. Collections of psalms were made under particular headings and used on special occasions. To make it possible to participate in the inexhaustible riches of the 'mystery of the psalms', anthologies were created. Individual verses from different psalms or indeed from all the psalms were put together in a new order from a particular perspective. From the Carolingian period on, this short psalter for private devotion and edification spread beyond the monastery and was used by educated people. St Francis was still familiar with its use. The office of the Lord's passion which he compiled is composed of a fabric of such psalm anthologies.

The degree to which the 150 Psalms (Psalter) were understood as the norm for prayer is made clear from the application of the term 'psalter' to patterns of lay prayer: for example, the saying of 150 Paternosters was known as 'the Paternoster Psalter'. The same goes from the 'Marian Psalter', i.e. the repetition of the Ave Maria, which spread rapidly after the twelfth century. In the course of the later Middle Ages the rosary was developed from Mary's greeting; it was regarded as a complete replacement for the Psalter and was propagated among the laity as the Marian psalter.

The additional offices created on the model of the main office in the ninth-century monasteries were imitated and increased in Cluny and the reform monasteries of the twelfth century. From the multiplicity of these additional offices the mendicant orders took over at least the office for the dead and the Marian times of day, and in the prayer books of educated lay people usually also the office of their own patron saint.

To avoid monotony in constant prayer, at an early stage the monks created appropriate physical and mental aids. For private prayer these were above all lorications (*lorica* = armour: originally thought of as a weapon in the fight against demons), i.e. physical gestures to accompany prayer by physical gestures. In the form of St Dominic's nine instructions on prayer, this practice, which had become customary in early mediaeval monasticism, was still current down to the late Middle Ages. The gestures could also be combined with new prayers or short exclamations. Early mediaeval monasticism also created material for this with verses from the psalms, ejaculatory prayer and brief invocations. These were constantly expanded and collected into litany-like prayers.

The countless litanies, hymns and prayers enumerated the holy and sanctifying properties of God. Under constantly new headings the material was constantly reshaped, and with alterations applied to the various mysteries of salvation: the Trinity, the individual persons of the Godhead, the incarnation, redemption, Mary, the saints, and so on. In later reordering and reshaping, for example appeals to the Holy Spirit became a petition for, or praise of, the seven gifts of the Spirit, and in a further step petitions for, or praise of, virtue. For example, in the 'greeting to the virtues', Francis of Assisi addresses the virtues as persons. His famous 'Hymn to the Sun' is also in the tradition of such exclamations of praise, which were taken over from the monastic world as '*laudes*' in the eremitical circles of central Italy during the twelfth century and given new form.

The different prayers were collected together in accordance with their basic content in the *precum libelli* (= prayer books of the Carolingian era) and handed down to the high Middle Ages. Although in form and content the material was rearranged from the second half of the eleventh century, the old *libelli* were still written out and disseminated under new names. This is true, for example, of the widely circulated 'Prayer Book of St Gualbert' (died 1073) and the Prayer Book of St Hildegard of Bingen (died 1179), written down in Cistercian convents in the first half of the twelfth century.

What is striking about the reorientation after the second half of the eleventh century is the move towards the life of Jesus, above all to the passion. The childhood of Jesus, the name of Jesus, the heart of Jesus, the five wounds, and so on became the object of special devotions. In the twelfth century, devotion to Jesus was accompanied by devotion to Mary, which again developed in a variety of forms and stimulated parallel literary creations (hymns, litanies, prayers).

The roots of the life-of-Jesus piety reach back into the monasticism of late antiquity. For the monastic discipleship of Jesus was always also a spiritual imitation in which the historical life of Jesus played a role. With this we should also connect the reformers' interest in the early church and the enthusiasm over the Crusades. With it the Holy Land became a religious theme which internalized monastic piety.

At all events, with its affective and meditative tone the life-of-Jesus piety brought enrichment and deepening. Anselm of Canterbury (died 1109), John of Fécamp (died 1078) and others were particularly active in stimulating it, and Bernard of Clairvaux was the great master. There were exercises in piety in the canonical foundations and the Premonstratensian and Cistercian monasteries of the twelfth century. The new writing was marked by spiritual breadth, a sympathetic disposition and sensitivity. This piety which drew on the higher level of education was freer and more personal in its expression, brought feeling and experience into play, and appealed to reflection and imagination. Its main theme became the longing to love God. The prayerful dialogues and monologues moved in a tension between human wretchedness and divine greatness, action and contemplation, knowledge and affect, understanding and love.

Whereas in the early Middle Ages an attempt had been made, for example, to invoke and enumerate the holy properties of God and the deficiencies and sins of human beings in long formulae of intercession and confession, now the same substance was expressed in affective and meditative terms. Invocatory formulae for protection became devotional meditative statements.

However, such an internalized imitation was not wholly new. It cannot simply be understood as a reaction to a recitation of formulae which had so increased in number. The external quantity of prayer in the early Middle Ages aimed at greater interiority. The admonition of the Rule of Benedict so to keep on praying the Psalms 'that our heart is in accord with the Word' (19.6) may be understood as a general monastic admonition. There is much evidence of it.

However, the goal of inner formation now became more deliberate and in a way was already regarded as methodical instruction. Albeit under different names, in the three stages of *lectio, meditatio* and *oratio* (or purification, enlightenment and union) all spiritual teachers aimed at intimate trust in God, dialogical openness to God, and an experience of God's presence.

The numerous treatises *de modo orandi seu meditandi* of the time aim to provide instruction in the experience of God. The spiritual writers of the mendicant orders continued this instruction. St Bonaventure's *Itinerarium mentis in deum* can be regarded as the classical summary of this tradition. In his great biography of Francis, Bonaventure combined St Francis' historicizing discipleship of Jesus with the doctrine of conformity to Jesus current in the monastic spirituality of the twelfth century. The great masters of the spiritual life in the twelfth and thirteenth centuries were teachers of mysticism, and their affective and meditative piety was a mystical one.

The term mysticism and what it refers to are used and explained differently in the history and philosophy of religion. Research into mediaeval mysticism since the nineteenth century has been strongly affected by this, and the result has been different explanations on which there is still no scholarly consensus. The philosophy of religion is interested in questions of the identity of being, i.e. of the participation of the human spirit in the absolute. The German Dominican Meister Eckhart (died 1328) in particular might be mentioned in connection with this speculative mysticism of identity. In the doctrine of being Eckhart followed Thomas of Aquinas, who emphasized the created nature of beings and grace, but in so doing combined Jewish-Arabic theology, cosmology and psychology with a Neo-Platonic philosophy of identity and the negative theology of Dionysius the Areopagite. Eckhart saw in the created sparks of the soul the ontic foundation for the divinization of human beings, who despite all inward illumination in the end are even more aware of the ineffability of the absolute divine mystery.

The Dominican's mystical philosophy of identity became a problem in the history of piety because of the supposition of a mystical school based on it. Dominican preachers and teachers were thought to have learned this mysticism in the German Dominican convents and to have produced an 'old German mysticism'. In the small amount of writing in which this is conveyed we can very clearly demonstrate the experience of a unity of identity of the spirit-soul with God, but there is hardly any indication of the mode of the union with the divine experienced in affect or will or even through reason. Furthermore, the mass of so-called mystical writings from the Dominicans, Franciscans and other women's convents of the time consists of traditional material from old monastic theology. In so far as high scholasticism transcribed these writings, the instructive and practical edifying element in them was even underlined further.

German 'women's mysticism', was not, as has been regretted, 'choked by a forest of authorities and the practical aims of edification', but lived by this writing, just as the scholarship of the time lived by texts and authorities. Nor may we forget that a monastery reached a significant spiritual level only if it followed the norm and forms of a rigorous monastic discipline.

However, as the earlier history of religion made a very sharp distinction between external and internal, spontaneous and controlled, utilitarian and ethical prayer, and dismissed the many monastic exercises as useless formalism, it felt compelled to look out for a special form of mystical writing which corresponded to its definition of mysticism as a simplification and totalization of interior prayer. But in reality this was the result of learning by heart. Constitutions and monastic customs prescribed it. The edifying literature which accompanied the prayer of the offices was the old monastic literature, even among German Dominican nuns.

All in all, the more intensive pastoral care of women in the thirteenth century had deep effects on piety. The widespread veneration of Mary and the canonization of various women (e.g. Elizabeth of Thuringia, died 1231, canonized 1234; Clare of Assisi, died 1253, canonized 1255; Hedwig of Silesia, died 1243, canonized 1267) helped to neutralize the devaluation of women which had been shaped by a long ascetic monastic tradition and supported by philosophical notions. Devotion to the life of Jesus in particular shaped the new women's piety and served as an example in the late Middle Ages. The biblical realism of the discipleship connected with this led towards the poor and the sick. In them people saw the poor man Jesus, to whom they turned out of compassion to help. Elizabeth of Thuringia, who was not content with alms for the poor, but went on to care for the sick, can be cited as an example of this piety. This care of the sick arising out of compassion for Jesus found a wide following in the Mantellatae (women as tertiaries of the various mendicant orders).

For enclosed nuns, conformity with Jesus was achieved in the framework of the monastic virtues of poverty, humility and penitence. Meditation on the passion, contemplation and vision, were the prominent characteristic of the ideal of the saints, and are attested by countless lives of nuns from the later Middle Ages.

3. The crusades and the fight against heretics

The crusades and the fight against heretics occupy a prominent place in the ecclesiastical and political actions of the popes of the twelfth and thirteenth centuries. They became important after the papacy had established its spiritual and ecclesiastical claim to precedence over kings. Thus the defence and dissemination of the faith had become tasks of the church. They belonged in the sphere of the material aspect of the spiritual sword of the church, at the disposal of which the secular authority had to place its temporal sword, to make the church's sword effective (cf. above III, d, ii). Both the crusades and the fight against heretics can be taken as test cases for this political theory. The various forces of the secular authorities obeyed the calls to crusades in the twelfth century and lent their 'arm' to the church in persecuting heretics. The Petrine apostolic principle found recognition and was at first accepted by the majority as an expression of the divine ordering of the world and salvation. But here, too, the pope's liegemen were able to combine their own interests with it, which ultimately led to quite different results from those envisaged at the beginning.

(a) The crusades: the church and war

The overall outcome of the crusades represented a terrible defeat, but they had unforeseeable effects. First of all, the West was again put in contact with the East for more than two centuries. During this time there were various Western feudal states in the Near East. For two generations the Latins also ruled Greek Byzantium. This geographical and political expansion led to a tremendous boom in trade of which the Italian cities made brilliant use, and on which Venice built its mercantile empire. Italy generally came back into the centre of political, economic and cultural activity, and this benefited the papacy in the twelfth century and was of fundamental importance for the development of the Italian cities. The encounter with Byzantium and the spiritual world of late antiquity which still lived on here broadened the spiritual horizon of the leading classes. This was even more true of the confrontation with Arab civilization and culture. Here special note should be taken of Aristotelian and Arabic philosophy, which only now was fully accepted by the West. The intellectual resurgence connected with this brought far-reaching changes to philosophy and theology. While it did not lead to any secularization of culture and society, the rationality of knowledge was extended.

The direct consequences of the first crusades were a tangible relaxation of the social tensions which had been produced by the marked increase in population (the development of cities and the rise of the lesser nobility). So the crusades also served to divert expansionist and social conflicts. Reflections on the holy war and the justified and permissible use of violence ultimately led to a monopoly of the use of force by royal power and to royal ordinances aimed at keeping the peace.

In religious terms the crusades introduced Jerusalem and the Holy Land into piety. They inspired the historicizing life-of-Jesus piety. They influenced piety in a cruder way by introducing many relics from the Near East, and more inwardly by the 'spiritual pilgrimage'; churches were built as copies of the earthly and heavenly Jerusalem and hospitals for those who took part in the crusades; and ascetic efforts were made to model the true Jerusalem in one's own soul. Finally there was a concern for the poor as the representatives of Jesus.

(i) The external course of history

In 1095 at Clermont Ferrand, Pope Urban II called on the 'Franks' to liberate the Holy Land, which had fallen into the hands of the Seljuks (since 1055 the Caliphate of Baghdad). The enthusiastic answer of his audience, '*Dieu le volt*' (God wills it), became the slogan of the enterprise which led to the First Crusade. All in all there were seven crusades aimed directly or indirectly at liberating Jerusalem.

The First Crusade (1096–99) was essentially the work of the French knights. Under Godfrey de Bouillon the army succeeded in capturing Jerusalem on 15 July 1099. In addition to the kingdom of Jerusalem, a series of further feudal states ruled by Western knights was established. After the loss of Edessa in 1144, Pope Eugenius III called for a new crusade, for which Bernard of Clairvaux in particular used his influence and eloquence. The

Second Crusade, in which the French king took part along with the German king Conrad III, ended in defeat. The Third Crusade was summoned after the conquest of Jerusalem by Saladin in 1187. Frederick Barbarossa, who took part along with other rulers, met his death on it in Asia Minor (10 June 1190). Egypt was the direct goal of the Fourth Crusade (1202–04). However, under the influence of Venice, the army turned towards Constantinople. In 1204 the city fell into the hands of the Latins. There was now an East Roman Latin emperor until 1261. Urban IV first withdrew support from him in connection with his anti-Hohenstaufen policy and again made an alliance with the Byzantine emperor. Innocent III was initially annoyed that the crusade had been diverted against Constantinople, but then accepted the facts as a welcome opportunity to impose the papal primacy of jurisdiction on Byzantium. The enterprise, inspired by Venice and then supported by the popes, led to an irreparable weakening of Byzantium over against the Turks. It intensified the already existing religious and eccesiastical dissent to hatred of the Latins in the population, on which all attempts at church union foundered.

The excommunicated emperor Frederick II carried through the Fifth Crusade (1228–29). It had begun with a campaign against Egypt (1218–21) which ended with a military defeat. Frederick II succeeded in restoring the kingdom of Jerusalem by treaty. In 1244 the Holy City was lost again, this time for good. Innocent IV called for its liberation at the Council of Lyons in 1245. However, the complications with the Hohenstaufens limited his power. So the Sixth (1248–54) and Seventh (1270) Crusades were enterprises of the French king Louis IX. The first campaign ended with his imprisonment in Egypt. He died on the second, which only took him as far as Tunis. In the meantime the enthusiasm for crusades had long since turned into a widespread sobriety and had given way to insight into the military inferiority of the Crusaders and the pressures of national aims nearer home.

In addition to these major enterprises aimed at Jerusalem there were also numerous individual actions, including irrational upheavals like the Children's Crusade of 1212, which met with a cruel end in

Marseilles. Thousands of children were fraudulently sold into slavery in Egypt.

The Iberian peninsula was a secondary theatre. The Spanish Crusades from the second half of the eleventh century onwards served to reconquer the land. Toledo was captured in 1085, Lisbon in 1147, Seville in 1248. Now only Granada was left to the Moors, and that did not become Spanish until 1492. In Spain the crusade became a war of conquest against unbelievers. In the twelfth century the same notion led in north-east Germany to crusades against the Wends and from 1230–83 to the conquest of East Prussia by the Teutonic Orders. From a crusade against unbelievers it was only a short step to armed combat against the enemies of the church and the heretics. The Albigensian Crusade in Southern France lasted from 1209 to 1229. Originally it was a fight against the Albigensians (Cathars), but in the end it led to the incorporation of Languedoc into the French kingdom. The idea of the crusade also inevitably appeared in the struggle with the Hohenstaufens. The popes declared them enemies and oppressors of the church and had the cross preached against them. By now the crusade had degenerated into a means of propaganda with which wars within Europe were legitimated.

In the fifteenth century the national Czech uprising (the Hussite Wars) and the expansion of the Turkish empire to the Balkans (Constantinople fell on 29 May 1453) led to a late and in effect vain revival of the idea of the crusade. The necessary papal initiatives were called for and welcomed by those immediately involved, but the Christendom of the late Middle Ages was no longer willing or able to engage in actions and defensive measures against the Turks which involved the whole of Europe.

(ii) Religious motivation – the justification of war

Two religious motives were decisive in the origin of the idea of the crusade: the pilgrimage to Jerusalem and the 'freedom of the church'. In the second half of the eleventh century, hosts of Western Christians were making pilgrimages to the Holy Land. The obstacles put in their way and the hostile attitude of the Seljuks led to the need for military escorts. The first step towards the crusade as an armed pilgrimage to Jerusalem had thus already been taken. The conquest of the Holy Sepulchre, Jerusalem and the Holy Land as the goal of an armed pilgrimage was rooted in the idea of the 'freedom of the church' put forward by the Gregorian reform. The church had to be snatched not only from the hands of simonists but also from the hands of unbelievers. So the earthly Jerusalem was seen as part of the church which had to be conquered for the freedom of God. Gregory VII already wanted to gather warriors under the banner of St Peter and lead them personally to Jerusalem in a 'holy war'. The complications of the investiture dispute prevented this from being carried out.

Military actions to protect and extend the faith were not new. In the church controlled by the nobility, however, they were tasks of the king, though of course the bishops and abbots also shared in them. Being a 'terror to the Saracens' played a role in the rivalry between the Byzantine and the Ottonian-Salian emperors. However, with the Gregorian reform the defence and spread of the faith became the task of the pope and the church. So war was to a degree 'ecclesiasticized'. The first crusades were thus something like an exercise in this new and hitherto unaccustomed role. In the course of the crusading movement a fundamentally new attitude arose to the use of force through military actions, which issued in the doctrine of the 'just war'.

To get this far, a series of moral theological objections had to be overcome. The thesis 'force must be repelled by force' was maintained, and was used to justify the use of force as a defence against acts of violence, as punishment of perpetrators of violence and as a deterrent against new acts of violence. However, any killing in the course of a military action of this kind was regarded as a transgression needing penance. The prohibition against killing and dissociation from the military profession as a legacy of the world-escaping asceticism of late antiquity influenced this penitential discipline.

The conflict could be resolved only if the moral theological evaluation of killing was made in terms of the intention of the killer and not in terms of the object, i.e. the action in itself. This move from an evaluation of the action to a moral theological dispositional ethic was made in theology in the course of the twelfth century. Here speculation was only catching up with what had already been anticipated in practice: the possibility of designating military action in the service of the church as a meritorious work (eventually, killing of the opponent was identified with punishment of the evildoer).

This new evaluation was prepared for by two related concerns: the protection of the church and the 'truce of God' (*Treuga Dei*). In the first instance noblemen banded together to protect a local sanctuary (usually a monastery) against violent attack. Possibly warlike action in pursuit of this aim was not only not regarded as an action needing penance but even seen as a meritorious work. Actions to protect the church of St Peter, the Roman church, were seen even more in this light. Particularly strong emphasis was put on the view of Gregory VII, and this was exploited for the benefit of the freedom of the whole church. Military action against simonist oppressors of the freedom of the church was justified in this way.

The 'truce of God', which is to be seen as a kind of peaceable ordering of the land before the emergence of the state, aimed at limiting feuds. For there was not yet a monopoly of the legitimate use of force against those who disturbed the peace. Disputes were not resolved by law but by recourse to weapons. The truce of God did not forbid feuds absolutely, but sought to introduce procedural rules and laid down conditions for a legitimate feud. The limited preservation of the peace which spread through France, especially from Cluny, and which was supported by the popes, could become effective only when those who broke the law and disturbed the peace could be punished by a 'peace troop'. Such military action which served to keep the peace was also regarded as meritorious.

Only through the approval of war in the cause of salvation which was expressed in these various stages were the conditions created for the (initially) enthusiatic assent of Western nobility to the crusades. A crusade for the protection of the church and the pilgrimage to Jerusalem – both meritorious works for the forgiveness of sins – combined the religious motive with the military action of the crusades. This also provided the possibility of combining the states of soldier and monk in the new orders of chivalry. It not only revalued the status of the military, which had formerly been suspect and required special penance, but also associated it with the monastic 'state of perfection'. In his *Liber ad milites de laude novae*

militiae, Bernard of Clairvaux enthusiastically celebrated the elevation of the warrior to becoming the soldier of Christ. Moreover the
knights could see their own ethos embodied in the orders of chivalry.
The combination of monk and warrior has to be seen against the
background of a political theory which combined the supernatural
order of grace and the natural order of law in a unity and gave the
priesthood competence in the order of creation as well as in the
order of redemption.

The Knights of St John, the Templars and the Teutonic Order
rapidly became significant. They were founded in connection
with the First Crusade, partly to look after pilgrims and the sick
and partly to protect them. A series of Spanish orders of chivalry
were limited to the Iberian peninsula: they were prompted right
from the start by military action.

The justification of warlike actions on behalf of peace and the
protection of the church gave the *sacerdotium* authority over war and
peace. So the priesthood (the pope) decided whether a war was a
'just war'. If it was, he granted indulgences to the participants and
thus justified them subjectively. His action made it permissible to
levy further war taxes on church property according to the principle
that those who defended the church should also be provided for
from church property. Since the interests of the pope and the rulers
coincided here, this caused no difficulty. However, in a conflict of
interest the rulers tried to to depict the papal position as an illegal
abuse of power, with propaganda to this effect.

The canon law doctrine of the just war had prepared them for this.
For the canonists of the twelfth century no longer looked at the just
war in terms of spiritual office but in terms of church property. For
them this was not a matter of the prophetic and theological
interpretation of history but a rational affair relating to the protection
of church property. Intrinsically, that was the responsibility of the
secular power, but because of the taint of sin the responsibility was to
remain with the priesthood. The secular legal scholars (legists) in the
service of their king rejected such a theological derivation of papal
competence and argued in terms of the needs of the realm. So the
just war was defined in terms of the common good. As the king was
responsible for the latter, the decision over war and peace also fell

within his competence. War became a legal instrument of territorial policy which no longer needed theological justification from the church, just as previously the religously motivated 'truce of God' had already been detached from the general ordinances of the king relating to the peace of the land. By the end of the thirteenth century the use of force had become a state monopoly. At this stage of the development the warriors did not need any church approval of their services by indulgences. The 'good' derived from the justice of the cause defended.

(b) Heresy and the fight against heresy

All questions arising out of the mediaeval understanding of heresy and the fight against heresy need to be considered in the light of the historical conditions. First of all, we should note the great degree to which the political realm and the church community coincided. This unity was the expression of the political form of religion which dominated thought and action in late antiquity and the Middle Ages down to modern times. Unity in confession and religious practice in this context was a constitutive element of any body politic. The elimination of religious dissent thus became a postulate of political reason.

The sharpness and urgency of the fight against heresy followed from the interpretation of salvation history. We therefore need to look at the concept of heresy. Heresy was understood as a fundamental contradiction to true faith and apostasy from it. True faith was interpreted as a fixed and unchangeable entity, which seemed to have no development or transformation. All attempts at development were *a priori* branded as heresy and even counted as demonology. The reduction of heresy to the 'work of the devil' made it dangerous to the community, and it had to be fought against with every available means. Thus the battle against heresy became part of the task of defending and deepening the faith. For heresy deeply affected not only the faith of the church but also the lives of believers. The eternal salvation of the individual was threatened, and the orientation of the community on eternal salvation was put in question. This linkage between salvation through faith and damnation through heresy obviously meant that fighting against heresy and warding it off was a public duty. Thomas Aquinas expressed this view in a simile: if a community punishes counterfeiters, how much more must it punish those who counterfeit the faith (*Summa Theologia* II–II q.11 a 3; cf. ibid., a.4).

Since sociologically speaking heretics were minorities and outsiders in society, as a rule they also encountered the malicious hostility of the majority to minorities. They were blamed for catastrophes and misfortunes. After the formal legal regulation of the punishment of heresy by the Inquisition, the pogroms which tended to develop did not so much affect the heretics as the Jews.

The pernicious global demonization of heresy which the Middle Ages willingly took over as the heir to late antiquity *a priori* put the heretics in the wrong. Christian antiquity had also made a catalogue of heretics available. Deviations from the consensus of faith and religious practice could thus be labelled and given a place in the heretical demonology.

(i) Heretical groups

In the concrete heresies of the time a distinction needs to be made between erroneous individual views and 'heretical popular movements'. The former belong predominantly in the intellectual milieu of the school. They were fought against or transformed by the disciplinary means of the monasteries or schools and the pressures of their system. In the great intellectual upsurge during the twelfth century, many teachers complained about being suspected of heresy. Real uncertainties about the application of the new rational methods and rivalries between schools were the background to this. However, none of the numerous 'school heresies' of the time got beyond the intellectual milieu. There was no popular heresy which was motivated and supported by the theology of the schools.

The various heretical trends among the people were supported by ascetic rigorism and a rural biblicism. Evidence of local social and religious acts of protest increases for the first half of the eleventh century. These protests were probably directed against the harmonious world of the church of the nobility. In the second half of the eleventh century, ascetic rigorism joined forces with the Gregorian reform in fighting the heresy of simony with which the system was said to be infected. In keeping with the new link between *sacerdotium* and *regnum* and the development of the papal church, ascetic rigorism turned against the secularized priestly church and called for a pure and poor apostolic church. The social and religious protest movement against the exercise of power and the life-style of the existing church spread with the Arnoldists, the supporters of Arnold of Brescia. In the course of the second half of the twelfth century, the opposition gathered around the Cathars and other groups.

The Cathars, also called Albigensians (after the city of Albi in southern France), formed the first organized anti-church of the Middle Ages. They reached the peak of their attraction towards the end of the twelfth and beginning of the thirteenth centuries. Internal conflicts and external persecution brought stagnation, which led to a rapid decline around the middle of the thirteenth century. The Cathar anti-church had a hierarchical constitution (with bishops). Its core was made up of the *perfecti*, who subjected themselves to the strictest asceticism, which in some circumstances could be intensified by a fasting to the death (*endura*). The ascetic merits of the perfect aimed at mediating salvation. The more committed adherents were the *credentes*, the believers, who by virtue of the ascetic merits of the *perfecti* could be sure of their salvation, and unlike them had material means at their disposal for the needs of the community. So formally the ascetic church of the Cathars shared the mediaeval understanding of the mediation of salvation. Doctrinally, however, its rigorism was accentuated to the point of becoming dualism in principle. We should see Eastern influences on this Manichaeism, which may have been communicated by links with Manichaean conventicles in the Balkans.

Though Catharism with its Manichaeism remained an indigestible alien body in the West, for the moment it made a great impression, and in some areas (like southern France and the cities of northern Italy) it attracted sympathizers from a variety of classes. There were two reasons for this. First, there was the widespread ascetic rigorism of the time, which had constantly attempted to connect the mediation of salvation in cult and sacraments with the ascetic life-style of the one who dispensed the sacraments. The second reason is political. Provisional toleration or encouragement of the Cathars could be used by the secular power to exert pressure on church claims reaching far into the secular sphere or to achieve the weakening of local church positions which was desired.

The early Waldensians might be mentioned as a revival movement within the church which was also opposed to the Cathars. The group which formed around Peter Waldo, a rich merchant from Lyons converted to an ascetic life of penitence, should be put within the religious penitential movement of the time, in which the eremitical ascetic ideal of the apostles had developed into an apostolic ascetic ideal. Its members lived lives of penance in keeping with the gospel and engaged in apostolic itinerant preaching. Scholars argue over whether in the case of Waldo the apostolic way of life (a radical renunciation of possessions) led to the demand for apostolic activity (itinerant preaching) or vice versa. At all events, Waldo's demand for freedom of preaching in keeping with the gospel brought him into conflict with the bishop. Their refusal to allow apostolic lay preaching forced Waldo and his penitential movement out of the constitutional church. In this emergency they resorted to the dispensation of sacraments by the laity and also departed from the church doctrinally. The rejection of the veneration of the saints, prayer for the dead, the doctrine of purgatory and so on came about less out of dogmatic considerations than from an ascetic rigorist concern for a strict life-style. This followed from their rigorist association of the validity of the sacraments with the ascetic holiness of those who dispensed them. Constitutionally, the Waldensians resembled a mendicant order the core of which was formed by the itinerant preachers, around whom loose conventicles of the enlightened and sympathizers formed. As a result of the persecution which began, the Waldensian conventicles were forced underground.

Within the range of popular heresies motivated by asceticism it is difficult to discover in detail what trend particular groups belonged to. The classifications of heretics by their opponents are not very useful for questions of this kind. However, the focal points and activities of the fight aginst heretics allow us to draw some conclusions about the dissemination of the popular heretical movement. With the development of the Inquisition into an effective instrument for fighting the heretics, any public influence had been made impossible. In so far as they avoided persecution, their supporters had to work underground.

The suppression of the ascetic popular heresies in the course of the thirteenth century is largely the result of the rigorous and carefully planned measures of persecution taken by the Inquisition. But in addition we should not overlook the pastoral activity of the mendicant orders, which, coming from the same ascetic tradition, had met the demands for asceticism in their life-style and also gave new impulses to piety. Here particular importance should be attached to the popularizing of the monastic life-of-Jesus movement, which combined abstract rigorism with vivid imagery and cold asceticism with religious warmth. We should also note a broad reintegration of revivalist circles which had become heretical into the life of church and society. The rapid spread and striking encouragement of the mendicant orders in the cities can be taken as clear evidence of this.

The complex range of these ideas in the transition to the later Middle Ages produced countless loose groupings and followers of the 'Movement of the Free Spirit'. Here ethical rigorism was combined with spiritualism and also with chiliastic enthusiasm. This is true above all of the Franciscan spirituals of the second half of the thirteenth century, who saw in Francis the dawn of the spiritual church of the eternal gospel. By 'eternal gospel' they understood the writings of the Cistercian abbot from Calabria, Joachim of Fiore (died c.1202). In his various commentaries on scripture, Joachim developed a doctrine of three stages in the history of salvation. The age of the Father (old covenant) led through that of the Son (the church) to the age of the Holy Spirit. In it, the priestly papal church would be dissolved and the sacraments of the church would be replaced by an outpouring of grace and knowledge. Stimulated by Joachim's numerical speculations on the duration of the individual kingdoms, Franciscan circles connected the calculations of the dawn of the 'third' kingdom with the work of the founder of their order.

The various conventicles and revival movements were always declared heresies when, like the Franciscan spirituals, they directly attacked the papal church and refused to obey it. However, as the demand for obedience reached far into the secular sphere, any stubborn rejection of spiritual power (in the form of the papacy) could be decreed a heresy. The Hohenstaufens and their Ghibelline supporters were vigorously accused of such politically conditioned 'heresy'. By the end of the development of the Petrine apostolic principle in the high Middle Ages this led to a disastrous narrowing of the concept of heresy.

(ii) The fight against heresy and the Inquisition

Mediaeval Christianity took over from late Christian antiquity the duty of warding off heretics and keeping the faith pure. It developed the traditional procedures further and created the Inquisition as a new defensive measure. In considering the development of the Inquisition we must note its historical context, its legal basis, its consolidation as an institution and its mode of procedure.

The occasion for its development was provided by the popular heresies after the second half of the twelfth century. Previously, heresy had not been a pressing problem of pastoral care. The existing mechanisms of suppression were enough to cope with the heresies of individuals in the intellectual sphere of monastery and school. From time to time popular deviations were dealt with according to the cautious principle of 'letting the tares grow until the harvest'. However, the *regnum*, which felt responsible for the external defence of the faith, dealt with any local religious or social movements harshly. Where deviant practices were felt to disturb the common good, there were also bloody atrocities against the people.

The massing of popular heresies, above all in the south of France, and their spread over large parts of Europe after the end of the twelfth century, resulted, under papal leadership, in the unification and tightening up of legislation against heretics.

Heresy was described as a crime tantamount to *lèse majesté* and a disturbance of the peace. So the fight against heresy served to keep the peace and could be carried on as a crusade. Collaboration in the detection of heretics and their punishment became a meritorious work. Death by burning was laid down as the punishment for stubborn heresy. In every case confiscation of property went along with this. Also punishable was refusal of legal help by the secular authority (the temporal sword, in the service of the church's material sword, see III, d, ii above), secret help for the heretics, or an omission to inform on them.

Legally speaking, the most important innovation was the replacement of the procedure under Germanic law with the Roman canonical process of interrogation. In the former the competent judge only intervened on the basis of an accusation (censure); in the latter, information was supplied with the aim of demonstrating the crime. Thus the public accusation in the process of censure became the Inquisition process (*inquirere* = investigate; *inquisitio* = investigation). In the fight against heresy, the bishop as the competent judge thus appointed *inquisitores* to track down heresies and bring those guilty of them before the episcopal court. However, the episcopal inquisitors do not seem to have engaged in a systematic search for heretics. Above all the bishops of southern France did not pursue their task very vigorously. At first the stricter legislation and the new procedure had little success.

This is probably why Innocent III resorted to the means of the crusade against the heretics, which the Third Lateran Council had already envisaged as an anti-heretical measure. The failure of the long Albigensian Crusade led Gregory IX to resort to legal proceedings. In 1231 he began to appoint inquisitors with far-reaching powers to individual church provinces troubled by heresy. These no longer had simply inquisitorial powers, but also functioned as judges. These inquisitors, acting on behalf of the pope were thus accusers and judges in one. By virtue of the omnicompetence of papal jurisdiction, Gregory IX also transferred to the inquisitors the power of pronouncing judgment. What was not clear was the relationship between these inquisitors, acting under special papal protection and commissioned by the pope, and the bishops. Blatant infringements of the law, transgressions of episcopal competence and the harshest inquisitorial practices in tracking down and condemning heretics led to widespread resistance and to a crisis in the newly created papal Inquisition between 1238 and 1241.

Under Innocent IV (1243–54) the courts were reorganized. Competences were made more precise and the procedure was regulated in detail. The most wide-ranging exemption from episcopal supervision was retained and the papal charge emphasized. Thus the *crimen haereticae pravitatis*, the crime of heretical evil, was treated as a special case which came under the pope, or presented as a substitute and emergency measure affecting the whole church, which had arisen out of papal concern. In terms of canon law and ecclesiology, behind the papal Inquisition lay the papal primacy of jurisdiction; in terms of church politics, the precedence of the *sacerdotium* over the *regnum*, in so far as the latter was no longer responsible for the external defence of the faith by virtue of its own dignity, as it was before the investiture dispute.

The fight against heretics only became effective with the appointment of delegated accusers and judges as papal inquisitors. After the reorganization under Innocent IV, limits had also been put to the arbitrary terror exercised by individual inquisitors, like Conrad of Marburg in Germany at the beginning of the 1230s. The proceedings were formally 'correct' by the standards of the legal and court procedures of the time (evidence in writing, a formal trial, etc.). Nevertheless, since the public were excluded, the work of the court could not be controlled and the accused had no rights whatsoever. As judge, the inquisitor was usually concerned to see his charges as prosecutor substantiated, and extracted a confession from the accused by torture. By nature the inquisition procedure amounted to a show trial in which the verdict was settled from the start because the procedure of itself usually led to the condemnation of the accused. The judges were prisoners of their procedure and were convinced that their task was legitimate and pleasing to God.

However, towards the end of the thirteenth century and even more into the later Middle Ages, the Inquisition which had spread so much terror could be effective only where the interests of the papal Inquisition, the bishops and the secular authority coincided. Here the original religious aim became combined with political, economic and social concerns. The beginnings of a transition to the state-church Inquisition can be detected.

Initially, the Inquisition was thought of as an emergency measure for a particular time and place. Some countries, like England, did not have a papal Inquisition at all; in others it proved transitory. By contrast, in France, Italy and Spain permanent institutions had already been set up in the thirteenth century with a prescribed range of competences. As heads of these institutions with their own houses, personnel and archives, following the practice of Gregory IX the popes largely appointed members of the mendicant orders. In the phase of development under Gregory IX these were primarily the preaching brothers with their academic training. They readily accepted their task and remained in office until it became a permanent position. At the end of the thirteenth century the majority of the inquisitorial courts had been entrusted to the Dominicans. In addition, of course, there were also inquisitors drawn from the secular priesthood and from other orders. Thus quite a few minorities were active as permanent inquisitors.

Both Dominicans and Franciscans soon made the task an aim of the order and saw their founders as the first inquisitors, active in this field 'to the greater glory of God and the increase of the faith'. This interpretation reflects a move to the legalized treatment of heresy. For here *potestas* (the power of the law) won out over *caritas* (pastoral care). Heresy was simply regarded as a crime which needed *coercitio* (punishment) and no longer laborious *persuasio*, i.e. preaching for conversion.

V

The Church in the Late Middle Ages

All in all, the late Middle Ages are a time of far-reaching changes in politics, the economy, culture and religion which after a slow preparation finally came to bear fruit towards the end of the fifteenth century. The results could be seen in scientific knowledge, which led to the 'Copernican shift'; the discovery of new continents and the broadening of horizons brought by this; the new feeling about life in humanism; and new political constellations in the European state system on the basis of territorial states which were now fully developed. None of the great cultures of the world experienced such a deep and far-reaching change in the course of its history as Western Europe did between the Middle Ages and modernity.

Historians put the transition to the late Middle Ages as early as the period between 1250 and 1300. The attack on Pope Boniface VIII (1303, see above, pp. 85f.) can be seen as a break here. The understanding of the Petrine apostolic principle in the high Middle Ages came up against resolute opposition from the forces which were determining the new time. In the course of the late Middle Ages, increasingly, though in different ways: 1. the claims of the papacy reaching far into the secular realm were forced back; 2. the papal claim to omnicompetence within the church was put in question; 3. the concept of the church and of church office connected with it was increasingly spiritualized and limited to the mediation of salvation.

The multiplicity of events in church history and the history of piety and the facts of church life in the late Middle Ages, which was so varied and is attested by such a horde of witnesses, can be ordered along the lines of these three tendencies. The first heading can be church government by the local ruler; the second, conciliarism; and the third, the individualization and internalization of piety.

1. *Church government by the local ruler*

The late mediaeval government of the church by the local ruler was not simply a secularizing emancipation of the royal power from the power of the papacy but a progressive participation of secular authority in church affairs. This ended with the widespread integration of the church system into the sphere of authority of a Christian form of government and its responsibility for the eternal salvation of its subjects.

The issue here was the control and supervision of the priestly mediation of salvation. For we should note as a legacy of the high Middle Ages to the whole of the late Middle Ages that the priestly mediation of salvation was not put in question. The generally undramatic process of participation and integration which took place in a mass of administrative ordinances and economic and financial steps was anti-clerical only in its suprastructure; in other words, it related to the authority and competence of pontifical authority in temporal matters. In mediaeval terminology, the issue under debate was not the priestly *potestas circa corpus Christi reale* (here in the sense of the mediation of salvation) but the *potestas circa corpus Christi mysticum* (here in the sense of the competence to rule over against the political structure of Christendom).

This process was not the result of a 'church struggle' which developed at random out of thin air, but is to be seen as a necessary consequence of the development of the *res publica* into the late mediaeval or early modern territorial state with its concentration of rule in the hands of its *princeps* (*magistratus*). In the course of this important process, step by step competence and authority were claimed by the local ruler, in whom rule was concentrated. The church institutions were primarily and particularly affected by this, but they were not alone. The whole exercise of rule in the feudal system with its manifold personal relationships and different legal competences was drawn in and transformed in sympathy.

Incorporation into local regional rule largely took place administratively. For with the concentration of statehood, new techniques developed in administration and jurisprudence. The exercise of administrative and legal control was systematized on a theoretical basis. A 'bureaucracy' trained in the law gradually developed, in which the clergy were increasingly replaced by lay officials. In this way there came into being at princely courts and among the city magistrates a new secondary level of government which no longer had any direct connection with church institutions, and which promoted the interests of its rulers; from the end of the fifteenth century it also sought new forms and content for piety and spiritual life. The beginnings of this new non-clerical class can be seen first in the Italian city states and at the courts of Frederick II of Germany and Philip IV of France. One of them, a legist partly despised by the church decretalists, Pierre de Flotte, argued in a controversy with Boniface VII: 'Your power is verbal, ours is real.'

The priesthood with its merely 'verbal power' had to implement its aims by collaborating with those who had real power. At the beginning of the fourteenth century, however, the rulers of Western Christianity were concerned: 1. to emphasize the independence of secular power; 2. to demonstrate their competence in the ecclesiastical sphere; 3. to show responsibility for the spiritual well-being of their subjects.

(a) The independence of the temporal

The 'temporal' is to be understood to comprise the whole public sphere, including the political, social, economic, cultural and spiritual ordering of a community (state). Here independence cannot yet be identiifed with 'autonomous worldliness' as though it amounted to emancipation from church norms and a laicization of state life. Independence from direct ecclesiastical intervention in the temporal sphere was the issue under debate. The competence of pontifical authority in worldly matters was to be cut back in favour of the individual states of Western Christendom; the possibilities of intervention in secular rule by reason of sin were to be eliminated. So the hierarchical superiority of the material spiritual sword was no longer to apply, or was to be redefined. All in all, this was a reaction against overdrawn hierocratic claims. For papal competence was further increased in the theoretical writings of the defenders of papal authority at the beginning of the fourteenth century in the face of the prevalent independence of national states which were emphasizing their rights. For this, reference can be made to writings like the *Tractatus de ecclesiastica potestate* of Aegidius Romanus (c.1302) and the *Summa de ecclesiastica potestate* of Augustinus Triumphus (died 1322). These were in part polemical works, written against the background of vigorous controversies. There had been clashes between Boniface VIII and Philip IV of France (1286–1314), and then again between John XXII (1316–34) and the German king Ludwig of Bavaria (1314–47). This last great clash between the papacy and the German (Roman) empire was also about the rejection of papal involvement in the election of the German king. The Declaration of Rhense (16 July 1338) pointed the way here: the one who is elected Roman king needs no approval, confirmation or assent from the apostolic chair. The view that the dignity of the German king derived from the pope was rejected as false.

As in all other conflicts, a stand was taken here on an authority which was not mediated by the priesthood but came directly from God. This view, too, was presented in polemical works and treatises. One of the earliest and most important discussions of this kind was the *Tractatus de regia potestate et papali* by the French Dominican Jean Quidort (written around 1302); the best known was Dante's *De Monarchia*, and the one which was sharpest in its polemical focus and boldest in its conclusions was the *Defensor pacis* of Marsilius of Padua (died 1342/43).

For all their differences, the basic tenor of these writings, which were important for the development of political theory, is the same: they all derive secular power directly from God. The argument is carried on in terms of natural law and through Aristotle's *Politics*. So the complete reception of Aristotle in the course of the thirteenth century was important not only for theology but also for politics. For the Aristotelian categories of thought gave the political theory of the time a means of working out rationally the difference between spiritual and temporal, *regnum* and *sacerdotium*, natural good and supernatural good.

This was not, however, simply a division of spheres, but a new connection between the natural and the supernatural common good. The immediacy of divine rule did not lead to a desacralization of rule but to its resacralization. For example, late German mediaeval princes ruling by the grace of God created sacral institutions for themselves in the cities in which they resided: court churches with collegiate chapels. So this was not the laicizing of rule and rulers, but their sacralization through participation in the 'holy' by virtue of their calling and task. In accord with this view, the emphasis on the independence of the temporal was combined with a progressive competence in the temporal ecclesiastical sphere.

(b) Responsibility in the temporal ecclesiastical sphere

The temporal ecclesiastical sphere is used here as a term denoting everything to do with the material substratum of the priestly *potestas circa corpus reale*. This was primarily church property. In a process of progressive participation, the authority acquired control over church property to the point of bringing it completely under the control of the local ruler. This was not a secularization of church property, an alienation of purpose, but supervision and trusteeship in keeping with its purpose.

There were theories to match this claim, too, centring on the question whether Christ had possession and dominion or whether he had only been given usage. In the Franciscan dispute over poverty the position of mere usage was vigorously advanced. In Ludwig of Bavaria's clash with John XXIII this became a fundamental issue. The theoreticians of poverty, of whom William of Ockham and Marsilius of Padua had made themselves the spokesmen, in principle denied that the priesthood could have possession and dominion and made it the duty of the secular authority to maintain the clergy who had been entrusted with priestly tasks.

Even more than this 'theoretical dispute over poverty', the facts themselves led to a progressive communalizing of church property. The process of progressive participation to the point of integration into the urban conditions of fourteenth- and fifteenth-century Germany can be demonstrated impressively. There was an urbanization of the church system everywhere. In some places this had already become comprehensive control of the church by the city by the eve of the Reformation.

The starting point for this process, which is so illuminating for the general tendency, was the efforts of the cities to gain autonomy, which aimed at full self-administration. In the long run even the church system could not be left out of the dispute. As things actually were at the beginning of the urban movement, the ecclesiastical institutions were occupied by the church of the nobility and protected from lay rule of the church by church law. The striking encouragement of the mendicant orders by the cities in the thirteenth century and at the beginning of the fourteenth created a first and important link between city and church and can be regarded as the beginning of the late mediaeval civic church. For at that time the churches of the mendicant orders were something like the secret parish churches of the urban corporations (see above pp. 97f., 99f.). An important step was then taken by the collegiate bodies which developed under private law: foundations for masses, funding for altars, schools, stipends, the care of the poor and so on. Each city council became a trustee for all this and thus succeeded in gaining control over things (resources) and persons (stipends). Responsibility for church buildings, in the form of taking over the cost of the buildings, was almost forced on the city corporations. For example, when in 1377 the city of Ulm moved the parish church 'in the fields' into the city and began building the minster, it pledged the patron (the monastery of Reichenau) that it would build the church out of its own means. Through the stonemason's lodge it thus gained control over the church. Then in 1446 the city purchased the whole patronage and thus as successor to the abbot of Reichenau gained full control of the property and income of the church.

Even in the old monastic or capitular churches, in this way cities gained control over monasteries and cathedrals, among them Strasbourg cathedral. Just as the court churches embodied sacral rule and validated that rule, so the confident awareness on the part of the city that it was a free and sacral community found unmistakable expression in the civic churches. Of course use was made everywhere of the possibility of providing finance through indulgences approved by the pope.

What applies to the communalizing of church property in the cities during the fifteenth century can also be extended to church government by the local ruler. As in the cities, here the hospitals took on a special function. And where the local ruler had founded a university, he could also use this institution for the same purposes. For both hospitals and schools were regarded as spiritual institutions which were therefore justified in using church property. With papal approval the local rulers transferred parish churches and other church posts to these institutions so that they could use the income. This policy of incorporation, which was mostly carried out systematically, not only provided material benefits but also contributed to the stabilization and extension of local rule. For the same reasons, the local rulers were particularly interested in monastic institutions. The protection of the local ruler and the patronage rights of monasteries tied these monasteries to their protectors and sponsors. The end result was the regional collegiate body tied to the local ruler with his different rights to control which were at the same time both spiritual and secular.

(c) Responsibility for the spiritual

The church policy of the authorities, aiming at integration through participation, also affected spiritual jurisdiction. The 'freedom' of church property and persons was limited step by step: control of the right of asylum by the authorities; the removal or restriction of freedom from taxation, to be replaced by the taxation of church property to finance public needs; the restriction of clerical jurisdiction and the increasing subjection of the clergy to civic jurisdiction to promote public order. In everyday life these claims constantly caused tensions and difficulties which fed an anti-clericalism. This was directed, in different degrees, against individual groups of clergy belonging to different social strata. Interdicts and other church censures which were against the interests of a city or a region were rejected as unjustified, and the authorities enforced a refusal to comply with them.

In the course of the fifteenth century the authorities gained increased influence on the public and private life of subjects by 'police and moral ordinances'. Peace and harmony, responsibility for the common good, were given as reasons in pronouncements in this area, which could take on the character of municipal sermons. Concern for what was 'useful and good for the city' also included care of public worship. For a view of political religion still held which associated the general well-being with God's will; God's grace could be obtained by the appropriate religious behaviour and God's punitive anger could be averted in the same way. In addition to control of the lives of subjects this included supervision of the clergy, not only of their life-style but also of their activity in worship and other spiritual matters. For the general good of subjects and the salvation of their souls it was necessary to supervise the priestly activity which conveyed salvation. Particularly in the cities, the authorities laid down conditions for the acceptance of pastoral charge. In many instances they required scholarly training for this. This concern for a 'Christian community' is also evident in increasing number of foundations by both private individuals and city magistrates to fund preaching after the second half of the fifteenth century. The donations from magistrates led to the appointment of city preachers who had to preach by virtue of their office.

The communalizing of the church system and the ecclesiasticization of the authorities was accelerated by emergencies within the church, first of all by the Western schism (see V, b,i above). In this emergency, for example the cardinals of Pisa (see below, p. 141) reminded the king of Aragon that it was the duty of kings and princes to note their rights in the church on behalf of believers and to proceed with force against those who divided the body of the Lord, i.e. the church, and his seamless robe. At the height of the clash between Pope Eugenius IV and the Council of Basel (see below, pp. 143ff.), numerous rulers adopted a neutral position: in other words, they did not recognize either the jurisdiction of the council or that of the pope. Such a refusal of obedience was ultimately based on the distinction between the church as a political body and the church as a mystical body: the former represented the external order and visible constitution, the latter the spiritual communion of believers with Christ, their visible head. The issue in the latter case was the authority of the church, i.e. the priestly mediation of the grace of the head (= Christ) to the members (= believers), but in the former only church government. In an emergency rulers could be responsible for this.

So the neutrality of the rulers resulted in a multiplication of the church system. From the end of the fourteenth century the question whether Christianity could not also have several heads had been raised here and there. The question itself could be meaningful only on the presupposition that the papal office was assigned merely responsibilities for external order and its competence was limited to church government, which had no direct connection with mediating the grace of the head. However, local rulers, too, could be responsible for ordering the church in such a way. At the beginning of the fourteenth century Wyclif had already spoken of a division of church government into many 'popes', and had written *ubi ecclesia, ibi papa*: where the church is, there is the pope.

But the English reformers understood the church to be a political community which was externally visible and structured by royal power. The head of this church was none other than the king. So the universal church as a body politic was to dissolve into the churches of the land, but remain invisible as a mystical body.

In theory such arguments were rejected up to the Reformation, but in practice the rulers increasingly became the proprietors of church government. The universal church was progressively parcelled up into different national churches.

In late mediaeval Christendom the church ecumenicity which had created the papacy of the high Middle Ages thus slowly faded away. This deeply affected its function. A reinforced state rule thus not only rejected claims put forward by the Petrine apostolic principle which extended into the political sphere, but with government of the church by local rulers in fact took away the substance of the ecumenical function of the papacy. In principle the Christian *res publica*, parcelled up into individual states, could order its church affairs even without the papacy.

2. Late mediaeval conciliarism

Late mediaeval conciliarism represented widespread opposition to the claim of the papacy to have some competence within the church which was guaranteed by the Petrine apostolic principle. The immediate occasion for this was the great Western schism. This was provoked by the election of two popes in 1378.

(a) Avignon and the schism

In a turbulent conclave between 7 and 9 April 1378, the college of cardinals first elected the Neapolitan Bartolomeo Prignani (Urban VI). In the course of the summer the cardinals had doubts about the legitimacy of this election, prompted both by the character of the man elected and the procedure in the elections. The cardinals abandoned Urban, and on 20 September 1378 elected the French cardinal Robert of Geneva (Clement VII). Since he could not remain in Rome, Clement returned with his cardinals and a majority of the members of the Curia to Avignon. The Curia had returned from this city in southern France, which with the county of Venaissin was part of the papal state, as recently as summer 1377.

The 'exile' in Avignon was primarily a consequence of the clashes between the French king and Boniface VIII. The Anagni attack (1303) had shown all the world that no independent or even hostile church policy could be pursued against the rising French nation state. An orientation on France seemed necessary. After the death of Benedict XI (7 July 1304), who reigned only eight months, in long-drawn-out negotiations the cardinals agreed on the Archbishop of Bordeaux, Bertrand de Got from southern France (who was elected on 5 June 1305). He was crowned pope as Clement V on 1 November 1305, but kept putting off the move to Rome. In 1309 he settled in Avignon with the Curia, which had previously resided in a variety of places. John XXII, elected pope on 7 August 1316 in Lyons after a vacancy in the see of more than two years and under massive pressure from the French king, would not dream of returning to Rome. So the Curia based itself on Avignon.

The French monarchy had an interest in this development and had played a part in it. Clement V in particular had become very largely dependent on the French king. So under pressure from Philip V he agreed to the condemnation and abolition of the order of Knights Templar. The general council summoned at Vienne (1311/12) served primarily to legitimate this infringement of law, which Clement had been ready to accept as the price for the annulment of the trial of Boniface VIII called for by Philip IV.

All in all, however, the Avignon papacy was not simply an extension of French interests but was intent on its independence.

However, the papal state could no longer be regarded as its material basis. After the departure of the Curia, its political and economic coherence collapsed and gave way to local rule. So the Curia sought to secure its independence by an appropriate financial policy. To this end, the beginnings already made in the course of the twelfth and thirteenth centuries were developed into a rigorous fiscal system. This amounted to the ruthless exploitation of the material resources of the church property of Western Christianity for the benefit of the Curia and its policy. To this end the reservations, provisions and expectations relating to church positions were extended, and a system of taxes and offerings (*servitia* and *annates*) was developed, along with a right to the disposal of taxes which could be implemented.

From the start, the fiscal system. which was constantly extended, provoked vigorous criticism and increased anti-curialism. The reason why the system functioned nevertheless and brought in considerable sums of money was that the interests of those concerned largely coincided. The fiscal exploitation of church property, to which pastoral interests were ruthlessly sacrificed, was thus not only significant for the Curia, but was equally practised by the subordinate church authorites and the local rulers in their own interests. More than anything else, this cartel of interests in the fiscal exploitation of church property and positions related to it shows the loss of moral substance and spiritual leadership suffered by the late mediaeval papacy. Step by step, the papacy had fallen victim to the 'secular influence' which initially it had sought to fend off by the reservation of positions and the like. In the end, the fiscalism of the local rulers proved stronger.

The immediate beneficiaries of the Avignon papacy were the countless employees of the inflated curial apparatus and the cardinals with their wide-ranging clientele of relations. The majority of the cardinals, most of whom had legal training and diplomatic experience, came from Limousin. In this way, through the Curia, a whole local establishment gained money, power and influence. These lords felt at home in the cultural and lively landscape of the south of France with its mild climate and relatively stable political conditions. They were not in 'Babylonian captivity'. That applied more to Rome, to which Gregory XI had ordered them after his return.

With the election of the Neapolitan Urban VI in April 1378, it was to be expected that the Curia would return to Italy, but this made the cardinals from the south of France rightly fear for their power and influence. Similar considerations were involved in the question of the legitimacy of the election of Clement VII. So it was natural to see the local preference for a French pope as the cause for the arguments, rapidly produced, about the compulsion and intimidation applied in the April conclave and the mistaken choice of candidate, which in the autumn then led to a new election. On these grounds, Clement VII had to be seen as the 'antipope'. But such a view of things does not go far enough. A pre-conciliarism among the cardinals was also a factor in the move to depose Urban and elect Clement, in which the cardinals sought a say in church government as 'part of the body of the pope'. However, Urban VI, with his own personal make-up, was neither willing nor capable here. In the end both parties stood by their principles and risked a break which led to schism. For the rulers rapidly decided for one pope or the other. Western Christendom was split into those who obeyed Avignon and those who obeyed Rome.

The effects of the schism became clearest in the increase in curial taxation, though this was connected with the considerable concessions to the pattern of church government by local rulers which was developing. Available church property had to be utilized to support two Curias. The Roman Curia, which in contrast to that of Avignon first had to organize an official apparatus, attempted to compensate for this lack, and systematically resorted to papal indulgences as a feature of fiscal exploitation. The jubilee indulgence for the Holy Year of 1400 was connected with this.

In cultic and religious terms, the direct effects were slight. For the priestly mediation of salvation was not affected by the schism. The pope of one obedience might have excommunicated the followers of the other, but the relevant rulers saw that the censures had no effect. So the schism was largely regarded as a matter of church politics, which had little to do with law and adminstration. Thus it was not so much the church as the mystical body of Christ which was affected by the schism, but rather the church as body politic. In this way, in the long term the schism encouraged both the spiritualization and the secularization of the concept of the church, which was not wholly unwelcome to the rulers. Only the supporters of an extreme papal concept of the church spoke of two completely separate churches. And mutual relations were not completely broken off. Negotiations continued, and there was a recognition of the unity of the church and thus of the duty to overcome the schism.

(b) Pisa – Constance – Basel

Various proposals were made for overcoming the schism. At a very early stage a council played a role in the considerations. After the failure of Benedict XIII and Gregory XII to achieve agreement, cardinals of both Curias adopted this course. In the Leghorn proclamation of summer 1408 they deposed both their popes and by virtue of their responsibility for the whole church as cardinals convened a council at Pisa on 25 March 1409. Both popes were put on trial, and in a conciliar conclave on 26 June, Alexander V was elected the new pope. He had a successor in John XXIII (1410–15).

The council's pope found the widest recognition in Western Christendom. But Pisa did not achieve complete unity, since parts of Christendom followed Gregory XII or Benedict XIII. Pisa probably failed because it acted too hastily against the two popes and impatiently put pressure on the cities of central Italy to acknowledge a papacy under Florentine influence.

However, Pisa had shown that a council was the best means of overcoming the schism. So a new council was needed, one which found the most widespread recognition among the European powers. The German king Sigismund (1410–37), at the same time king of Hungary and Bohemia, was especially in favour of this. Moreover, he had exerted pressure on John XXIII, who finally convened the council at Constance on 1 November 1414. The pope elected at Pisa may have hoped that the assembly at Constance would help him to gain general recognition. However, when it emerged that the council would ask him to resign for the sake of unity, on 20 March 1415 he suspended the council and fled from Constance. In this emergency, in which the continuation of the council was at stake, the conciliar mood became increasingly self-confident. It found expression in numerous opinions and sermons, above all in the council decree *Haec sancta*, which was passed on 6

April 1415. The council defined itself as a representative of the church which had its authority directly from Christ, and which 'everyone, of whatever state and dignity, even that of the pope' was obliged to obey.

From then on the council pursued its agenda on its own responsibility: the *causa fidei* (Hus), the *causa reformationis* (the reform decrees) and above all the *causa unionis*. Processes demonstrated to the three popes that their office was not valid. John XXIII was deposed on 25 September 1415 and Benedict XIII on 26 July 1417. Gregory XII had avoided condemnation and had resigned on 4 July 1415. A new election did not take place until November 1417. On 11 November the Roman cardinal Odo Colonna was unanimously elected pope as Martin V (1417–31). This ended the schism, and Western Christendom again had a supreme head who was universally recognized. Conciliarism seemed to have stood the test and to have proved a guarantor of church unity.

The conciliarism practised in Constance had become more sure of itself and took its stand on the council as the permanent constitutional institution of the church. In the decree *Frequens* passed on 9 October 1417 it committed the popes to holding regular councils (a first council after five years, then one after seven years and thenceforward one every ten years; this was passed along with four further reform decrees). The important decree was intended as a means of also involving the pope and the Curia in church reform. But it could hardly be assumed that the papacy, which owed its regained universal validity to the council, would in the long run accept such restriction and control. So the next conflict was pre-programmed.

Martin V, who concluded the Council of Constance on 22 April 1418, summoned the next assembly at Pavia in accordance with the wording of *Frequens*. In the summer he transferred the council, which was opened on 23 April 1423 and was sparsely attended, to Siena, and dissolved it again on 19 February 1424. The unresolved *causa reformationis* was to be discussed at the next council, planned for Basel in 1431. So Martin V observed the letter of *Frequens*, but at the same time prevented the synod from being effective. He even exploited what might be termed 'synodical fatigue' and relied on the permanence and greater efficiency of the Roman Curia, which was to make the council seem superfluous.

Eugenius IV (1431–47) resolutely continued these tactics. Granted, he first confirmed the council, which met in Basel in the summer of 1431. But on 12 November 1431 he dissolved it out of hand and planned another in Italy, at which there were to be negotiations with the Greeks over a union. In contrast to Pavia-Siena, this step taken against the meaning and wording of *Frequens* caused indignation among the members of the synod. They remained together and demonstrated conciliar self-assurance. Under the pressure of the secular powers, above all Emperor Sigismund, who were not interested in a break between pope and council, Eugenius fell into line and recognized the council again on 15 December 1433. Meanwhile the conflict simmered on, and broke out once more in connection with the planned transfer of the meeting place for negotiations over union with the Greeks. On 30 May 1437 a minority of the council, pro-Eugenius and pre-dominantly consisting of Italians, voted to transfer it to an Italian city. Eugenius snubbed the majority, confirmed the vote of the minority, and on 8 January 1438 opened the union council with the Greeks in Ferrara. Union with the Greeks was achieved in the bull *Laetentur coeli* of 6 July 1439. Granted, this reunion largely existed only on paper, but for the moment it could be utilized as propaganda against Basel. It could be proved to all the world that the pope's council, and not that in Basel, had brought about the unity of all Christendom. Clearly this damaged the prestige of Basel.

The council, forced on to the offensive, now insisted even more on conciliar principles. It referred to *Haec sancta*, and interpreted it in the decree *Sicut una* of 16 May 1439 in terms of a strict superiority of the council to the pope. The 'three truths of the Catholic faith' put forward in this degree (1. that the council stands above the pope; 2. that the pope may not transfer or abolish a council without conciliar consent; 3. that any stubborn resistance to these principles is to be regarded as heresy) were also intended as an instrument against Eugenius IV. On 24 January 1438 the council had suspended him from office. The process which was opened against him in early summer 1439 ended with his deposition as a 'stubborn heretic and schismatic' on 25 June 1439. On 5 November 1439 the council chose a new pope: Count Amadeus of Savoy (Felix V). However, he had no special interest in the new schism, which had largely come about because the council had gone its own way without the encouragement of the secular powers. On the whole people waited, or declared their neutrality, supporting neither Basel (and its pope) nor Eugenius IV. In countless negotiations and attempts at mediation the idea of a 'third council' was also discussed. The diplomatic skill of Eugenius IV and ambassadors like Nicholas of Cusa or Enea Silvio de Piccolomini succeeded step by step in persuading rulers to recognize Eugenius or his successor Nicholas V (1447–55). On 7 April 1449 Felix V resigned, and on 25 April the rump council, transferred from Basel to Lausanne and long isolated, dissolved itself. 'Basel conciliarism', and with it conciliarism generally, seemed to have failed and to have been refuted by the papacy. For the renewed division was not overcome with a council, but in the face of the council.

(c) The development of conciliar theories

One can hardly talk about unitary conciliar theories in the late Middle Ages. There were different conceptions and aims with an abundance of overlapping nuances. In considering any question of detail we need to note the legal background. Just as the mediaeval papacy was a matter of jurisdiction, so too was conciliarism. It was about the authority to decree binding norms for the doctrine and life of the church, not by virtue of an ecclesiastical 'sovereignty of the people' of whatever form, but by virtue of the divine legitimation of church officials. The conciliarism of the late Middle Ages was not developed from notions of popular sovereignty and then introduced into the church as a heretical alien body, but had its roots in the canon law of the high Middle Ages. This developed a corporative and juridical understanding of the church comprising notions which necessarily led to conciliarism.

To secure the freedom of the church from the proprietary church of emperor, king or nobility, canon law attempted to define the superstructure of the church with notions of corporation theory. So it defined church institutions as moral persons justified in acting and capable of rule. Accordingly, for example the bishop together with the cathedral chapter formed such a corporation, which was regarded as a representative of the 'church' (= diocese) under it, on behalf of which it could act. This whole (*totum*) consisted of head (bishop) and members (members of the chapter). The bishop was the authorized head and special representative of the corporation. But as head, he too was obligated to the whole, because this was where authority rested. This mutual relationship was expressed by various axioms like 'the whole is greater than its part' (*totum est maior sua parte*); 'let what affects all be approved by all' (*quod omnes tangit, ab omnibus approbetur*), etc.

In the same way, the college of cardinals understood itself as a corporation of the whole church with the pope as its head. However, this preconciliarism of the cardinals, which amounted *de facto* to an oligarchical church government, was exposed to a twofold tension. One side affected relations with the pope, the other relations with the whole church. This tension was manifest in the schism. The cardinals who had risked schism because of their responsibility for church government had to call on the whole church to overcome it. So the pre-conciliarism of the cardinals led to the actualization of a conciliarism of the whole church.

Initially, the canon law of the high Middle Ages had also described the whole church as a corporation: the pope as head and the bishops as members. It was all these together who formed the whole which as such was greater than its parts. According to the corporative conception, the authority resting in the whole was transferred to the pope on his election, so that the pope was understood as 'delegate' and 'minister' of the whole church. Such a delegation of authority was not seen as contradicting either appointment to the Petrine office by Christ or the monarchical rule of the pope. For while Christ had transferred the same spiritual powers to all the apostles (= bishops), he had given a far superior commission to Peter (= the pope). The pope was to define and limit the intrinsically unlimited authority of the individual bishops for the sake of unity and order to form a particular church.

However, this understanding of the role of the papacy in ordering the church, formulated in terms of a corporate law which was only partially developed, was overlaid by an approach in terms of the law relating to persons. This seemed to correspond better to the Petrine apostolic principle. In the latter conception there was a sharp distinction between the power of order and the power of jurisdiction.

Whereas Christ had given the power of order to all apostles (= bishops), he had entrusted jurisdiction only to Peter (= the pope). So all ecclesiastical jurisdiction derived from the pope. There was no place in this conception for a corporate overall authority. Accordingly, in electing a pope the electors had only to nominate the particular bearer of the fullness of power mediated by Christ; they did not delegate anything to him. Thus corporate and personalistic understandings of jurisdiction in the church were sharply opposed. However, this fundamental dissent was masked by the dispute between *regnum* and *sacerdotium* and by the extension of spiritual power far into the secular realm, which also benefited the bishops. So it was not a specific issue in controversies. Episcopal resistance occasionally developed in the course of the second half of the thirteenth century, and became more massive in connection with the criticism of the Avignon fiscal system; the personalist juridical concept became a fundamental problem with the schism. In the context of the councils people again began to reflect on the understanding of the church as a corporation, sharpened it, and developed it further in the conciliarism of Constance.

Here canon law provided help at an important point. The famous decree *Si papa* (*Decree of Gratian* d.40, c.6), much cited by the canonists, made it clear that the pope could not be deposed, but this was qualified by the heresy clause (*nisi deprehenditur a fide devius*). This indicated that in matters of faith the exempt position of the pope remained limited, i.e. bound to the whole church. The commentators indicated the council as the appropriate forum for establishing whether a pope had erred in the faith. Under the pressures of the schism the concept of heresy was extended: the stubborn refusal of a pope to surrender his office in favour of unity convicted him of a proneness to heresy, i.e. a denial of the unity of the church.

Thus the personalist understanding of the papal office had again been overtaken by the corporate understanding at the level of faith. For in the general view of even the moderate 'papalist' theologians and canonists of the time, while the pope was greater than the church in his government of the church, he was not so with respect to faith. So in the matter of faith the pope was subordinate to the whole church. If the head of the church erred in this matter, which was fundamental to the church, the church had to intervene and see to a new supreme head. So the superiority of the pope in the government of the church did not rule out his inferiority at the level of the faith.

The decree of Constance, *Haec sancta*, might also be seen against the background of this 'conciliarism of the tradition' rather than being understood as a document of an absolute superiority of the council. Pope Eugenius and his followers branded *Haec sancta* as a statement which (heretically) set the council above the pope; the Basel council stylized it as an (orthodox) confession of the absolute supremacy of the council. In both cases the wider church framework of the relationship between pope and council was torn apart with different co-ordinations and subordinations and intensified so that it became an opposition relating to both the faith and the government of the church.

Sicut una of 1439 referred explicitly to *Haec Sancta*. In reality the 'three truths of the Catholic faith' were the expression of the flickerings of a different conciliarism. In the extraordinary situation of three popes, the Council of Constance was given widespread assent by Western Christendom. In *Haec sancta* Constance could rightly claim to be the sole representative of the church as a whole. When Basel issued the decree *Sicut una* in 1439, it lacked such widespread assent. Moreover in Eugenius the council was dealing with a legitimately elected pope, whose deposition found little recognition. In order to legitimate itself in the face of this decline in assent, Basel understood itself as a representative of the whole church by divine appointment, without reference to the consensus of the church as a whole. On the basis of the postulate 'where the council is, there the church is' (*ubi concilium, ibi ecclesia*), it called for simple obedience; in the case of the pope, it called for obedience not only in matters of faith but also in matters of government. For in this understanding of council and church in principle there was no place for a head of the church ordained by divine right. The papal office was merely responsible for ordering the church on its behalf.

The majority of Western Christendom was not prepared to follow such a concept of the council, which was no longer guaranteed by tradition and which above all went against the situation in church politics.

However, the widespread dissent with Basel should not be confused with a departure from the 'conciliarism of the tradition'. Councils still stood in high esteem, above all as a means of reforming the church, head and members. But Pope Eugenius and his followers attached the utmost importance to bringing conciliar thinking generally into disrepute along with Basel. They vaunted themselves as victors in the face of conciliarism. In reality they were also losers. For Eugenius IV and Nicholas V purchased their general recognition by the European rulers at a high price. In the various agreements they conceded those areas of responsibility which consolidated the government of the church by local rulers and advanced the further parcelling up of Western Christendom into regional churches.

3. Piety is individualized and turns inward

In structural terms, the religious and ecclesiastical practice of the later Middle Ages simply continued forms which had been developed since the early and high Middle Ages. However, in the meantime this piety had been disseminated more widely, and through the activity of the mendicant orders and other pastoral efforts had reached the lower classes with their customary usages and popular piety. In this way, on the one hand the piety was ecclesiasticized, but on the other hand archaic and primitive forms of religious practice found their way into the church's piety to a massive degree. It has to be said that the late mediaeval church lacked the power and the will to purge, discipline and integrate this popular piety. Thus although late mediaeval piety was established on a broader basis, hardly any new ideas were developed in it. What was striking was the quantitative increase in practices. There was an increase in pilgrimages and the veneration of saints and relics; in eucharistic devotion which attached much importance to the visual dimension, to seeing, carrying round and displaying the host (monstrances); in donations and bequests provided for masses and altars; and in a great many other good works. Given further value by indulgences, these occupied an important place in individual piety as contributions towards a favourable heavenly 'balance sheet'.

Such an excessive materialization and quantitative increase inevitably provoked a reaction and created a need for simplification and concentration. The mannered luxuriance of forms and themes thus already threatened to cause satiation. The 'iconoclasm' of the Reformation was a counter-move in this dialectical relationship of externalization and interiorization. But this change, too, had its prehistory, which belongs to the piety of the late Middle Ages. For increasing indivualization and interiorization accompanied this externalization. The interweaving lines of development can be described under the headings of edifying literature, *Devotio moderna* and religious humanism.

Edifying religious literature played an important role in the literary education of the late Middle Ages. This religious literature spread widely in the fifteenth century, first through manuscripts and then, from the second half of the century, through printing, the invention of which must be seen as an important precondition for more widespread literary education. Here literature in the vernacular increasingly came to the fore. Earlier scholarship saw this as a symptom of the growing emancipation of piety from its ties to the church and the clergy and the beginning of a secular and independent lay piety. But such a view fails to do justice to the persons involved in the development and its structure. For most religious writings were produced in the milieu of the clergy and the church; above all the old monastic traditional material used for edification and the teaching material used in the schools was translated into the vernacular or rewritten in it. So the sociology of literature, research into its public and the history of the reception of individual literary genres do not attest a laicization of religious education but indicate the interest of broad and educated lay circles in participating in the exalted monastic and ascetic piety of tradition. The new literature was addressed to the individual; its concern was personal devotion and a virtuous life. The religious literature which had an influence beyond the monastery thus reinforced the shift towards the individualizing and interiorizing of piety. Treatises intended for personal reading like Heinrich Suso's *Horologium sapientarum*, Thomas à Kempis' *Imitation of Christ* and the numerous books of consolation and self-examination had a very wide circulation. The same is true of invitations to personal devotion like reflections on the life of Jesus, Mary, the saints, and on death, and of the Books of Hours.

The *Devotio moderna* which came into being in the Netherlands at the end of the fourteenth century and had an influence well into the next century is to be included in this general trend, which was most pronounced at the level of literary education. Similar concerns in other regions and spiritual centres need not necessarily have been influenced by the *Devotio moderna* or even be dependent on it. The *Devotio moderna* was not unique in its ideal and its invitations to piety. The level of literary education and corresponding religious praxis was maintained. There was an emphasis on pious inwardness, keeping outward forms at a distance. The ideal was to cultivate the virtuous life in silent retreat from the world. The claim to be living a monastic life without binding oneself by vows was a new one. At the beginning of the fourteenth century the same concern had led to the condemnation and persecution of the Beguines, local associations of women leading a religious life, predominantly in Germany and the Netherlands; now the idea was recognized by the church. This change is significant and illuminating. The notion that intercessory prayer had to be offered by ascetics (monks) who had renounced the world, since the laity were incapable of perfection and comprehensive sanctification because of their roots in the world, had been a basic element of the piety of the early and high Middle Ages. Now this was broken through by the 'new piety'. The monastic life as defined and fixed by law was interpreted as one of the ways to perfection, and no longer as an embodiment of the perfect life.

This notion then completely dominated the religious humanism of the later Middle Ages. Humanism as a whole is something over which scholars argue. We need to note the many different forms it took, the chronological development from the end of the fourteenth to the sixteenth century, and the different regional manifestations. Humanism, with its concerns for literary education and reform, can no longer be described as an anticipation of the emancipation of the Enlightenment. The links with the Middle Ages cannot be overlooked. Often the old was carried on in the new, and no clear dividing line can be recognized. Often the new simply broke through the form of the tradition and not its content. Nor was religious humanism utterly opposed to scholasticism. The neo-scholasticism of the beginning of the sixteenth century with its intense study of Thomas in Italy and Spain was powerfully stimulated by humanism. We should also note the impulses in the relationship between late Scholasticism and humanism which derived from the theology of edification and proclamation at which Jean Gerson's efforts at reform were directed.

Fed by various sources, at the end of the sixteenth century the ideal of piety then took a new form in religious humanism and found new criteria in the church fathers and holy scripture. This piety, deepened and supported by education, also trusted more in the direct illumination of the Holy Spirit than in the magisterium of the church. Of course the magisterium did not immediately come under criticism; but traditional forms of religious practice like pilgrimage, the veneration of saints and indulgences were criticized as superstitious externals.

The new 'religious openness' was disseminated by a great variety of writings and personal contacts. The audience was above all the educated in the cities and at the courts, who formed a new subsidiary ruling class. In form and content this was already the outline of a piety in which individuals assured themselves of their salvation, existing alongside the clerical administration of the sacraments. So further impetus was needed before the mediation of salvation through the church and the pope were put in question. The widespread positive response met with by the Reformation concentration on faith alone and the simplification of piety to 'scripture' alone had been prepared for by the individualization and interiorization of the late Middle Ages. However, this concentration and simplification which took place everywhere under the influence of religious humanism did not necessarily lead to the church of the Reformation, but could also happen within the old church. That was shown by the Catholic renewal movement in Romanic countries like Spain and Italy.

Bibliography

B. Bolton, *The Mediaeval Reformation*, Edward Arnold 1983

R. and C. N. L. Brooke, *Popular Religion in the Middle Ages*, Thames and Hudson 1984

C. M. D. Crowder, *Unity, Heresy and Reform, 1378–1460*, Edward Arnold 1977

C. Erdmann, *The Origin of the Idea of the Crusade* (1935), Princeton University Press 1977.

J. N. Hillgarth, *The Conversion of Western Europe, 350–750*, University of Pennsylvania Press[2]1986

George Holmes, *The Oxford History of Mediaeval Europe*, Oxford University Press 1992

E. LeRoy Ladurie, *Montaillou*, Penguin Books 1984

C. H. Lawrence, *Mediaeval Monasticism*, London 1984

Hubert Jedin and John Dolan, *History of the Church*, Vol.III, *The Church in the Age of Feudalism*, Burns and Oates and Crossroad Publishing Company 1980

Hubert Jedin and John Dolan, *History of the Church, Vol.IV, From the High Middle Ages to the Eve of the Reformation*, Burns and Oates and Crossroad Publishing Company 1980

J. N. D. Kelly, *The Oxford Dictionary of Popes*, Oxford University Press 1986

David Knowles and Dimitri Obolensky, *The Middle Ages*, The Christian Centuries, Vol.2, Darton, Longman and Todd and McGraw-Hill 1969

H. E. Mayer, *The Crusades*, Oxford University Press 1972

Bernard McGinn, *The Growth of Mysticism. From Gregory the Great to the Twelfth Century*, Crossroad Publishing Company and SCM Press 1995

Bernard McGinn, John Meyendorff and Jean Leclercq (eds.), *Christian*

Spirituality I. Origins to the Twelfth Century, Crossroad Publishing Company and SCM Press 1989

R. I. Moore, *The Origins of European Dissent*, Allen Lane 1977

K. F. Morrison, *Tradition and Authority in the Western Church*, Princeton University Press 1969

D. E. Nineham, *Christianity Mediaeval and Modern*, SCM Press 1994

Jill Raitt, Bernard McGinn and John Meyendorff (eds.), *Christian Spirituality II. High Middle Ages and Reformation*, Crossroad Publishing Company and SCM Press 1989

Y. Renourd, *The Avignon Papacy 1305–1403*, Faber 1971

J. Riley-Smith, *The First Crusade and the Idea of Crusading*, Athlone Press 1986

R. W. Southern, *Western Society and the Church in the Middle Ages*, The Pelican (Penguin) History of the Church, Vol. 2, Penguin Books 1970

Walter Ullmann, *A Short History of the Papacy in the Middle Ages*, Methuen 1972

J. M. Wallace Hadrill, *The Frankish Church*, Oxford University Press 1983

Anton Wessels, *Europe: Was it Ever Really Christian?*, SCM Press 1994

The Oxford Dictionary of the Christian Church, ed. F. L. Cross and E. A. Livingstone, Oxford University Press 1974, provides a wealth of information (a third edition, edited by E. A. Livingstone, is in preparation).